SECRET
ESOTERIC CHRISTIANITY

*The Two Marys, the Two Families of Jesus,
and the Incarnation of Christ*

GILBERT CHILDS

TEMPLE LODGE

Temple Lodge Publishing
Hillside House, The Square
Forest Row, RH18 5ES

www.templelodge.com

Published by Temple Lodge 2005

A catalogue record for this book is available from the British Library

ISBN 1 902636 73 2

Cover design by Andrew Morgan, featuring *Holy Family* by Bernart von Orley
Typeset by DP Photosetting, Aylesbury, Bucks.
Printed and bound by Cromwell Press Limited, Trowbridge, Wilts.

We must unite faith with knowledge: faith alone is not sufficient, but backed up by spiritual-scientific concepts, the combination of the two leads to genuine wisdom rather than unconnected parcels of information.

Rudolf Steiner

Books by the same author:

Steiner Education in Theory and Practice
Education and Beyond
Rudolf Steiner, His Life and Work
The Realities of Prayer
Understand Your Temperament!
Balancing Your Temperatment
Your Reincarnating Child (with Sylvia Childs)
From Birthlessness to Deathlessness
5 + 7 = 12 Senses
An Imp on Either Shoulder
The Journey Continues ... (with Sylvia Childs)
Truth, Beauty and Goodness

CONTENTS

PREFACE

The contents of this book may well be regarded as heretical by many readers, but it is quite likely that, having read it with an open mind, they may then regard orthodox or received Christianity as dissident. When at Christmastide Christians old and young celebrate the birth of a very special baby, most merrymakers do not realize that the grounds for doing so are very shaky. Little do they know that the carols they sing pertain for the most part to the baby Jesus mentioned by Luke in his Gospel, regardless for the most part of the nativity story to be found in Matthew's Gospel, which is much shorter and altogether different in character and content. Theologians and other interested Bible readers have, over many years, attempted to reconcile the utterly different nature and contents of these two contradictory accounts, but orthodoxy settled on that of Luke. However, a valid explanation of their glaring discrepancies was arrived at by Rudolf Steiner, whose findings regarding the whole affair are at once biblically enlightening and convincingly sound.

It is widely held throughout Christendom that the child born in Bethleham was 'Jesus Christ', that is to say, as truly divine as well as human in nature. Such a conviction seems not to be so firm, however, if reference be made to the baptism of the man Jesus of Nazareth in the River Jordan by John the Baptist, when God himself declared: 'Thou art my Son, my beloved; on thee my favour rests.' But it is all too little known that 'some witnesses read *My son art thou; this day have I begotten thee*' (Luke 3:22, New English Bible). Now those readers who accept this are known as 'Adoptionists', that is to say, their conviction is that God's son was *adopted* at the time of his baptism as Christ, and not at his natural birth as Jesus.

This important event along with related 'heresies' will be discussed in the course of this book. Readers will be encouraged to look behind what to some are mere biblical annals and obtain enlightenment and deeper understanding of the message of the Gospels. This book provides ample food for thought; but it is strong meat, not milk for babes.

1
WHAT IS ADOPTIONISM?

Being invisible in his own nature, he became visible in ours
St Leo I (Pope 440–61)

The nature of Christ Jesus

A working definition of Adoptionism (or Adoptianism) is the doctrine or belief that Jesus of Nazareth was appointed to be, or adopted as, the Son of God after his 'birth'—that is to say, at some time between then and his death and resurrection. The basis for the notion of Adoptionism is its denial of the firmly held traditional belief that the Incarnation, the union of divinity with humanity as manifested in Christ Jesus, occurred at the time of conception.

The whole highly contentious affair was a matter of fierce argument in the early years of the establishment of Christian doctrine and practice, and emphasis was increasingly placed on the role and status of the 'Virgin' Mary as the mother of the individual known as Jesus Christ. This notion is as absurdly remarkable as it is deluded. Scant attention has been given to certain biblical texts and/or their interpretation, which has resulted in an increasing lack of their entire acceptance and thus given rise to erroneous doctrines and beliefs. Orthodox teachings totally ignored the fact that there were indeed two Jesuses, two Marys and two Josephs, as witness the discrepant accounts concerning these individuals appearing in the Gospels of Matthew and Luke, of which more anon. It is clear from the Gospel texts that there were two entities which by some means became one, and were two beings of differing origins, namely, Jesus of Nazareth the human being, and (the) Christ, who is presented in the Gospels as 'Son of God'. This is a weighty problem, which has been shamefully averted by successive generations of scholars and religious factions for as long as Christianity has existed, and it must be addressed.

Now this whole matter insists on the presence simultaneously of two natures: the divine represented by the Messiah or Anointed One, and Jesus the human being. This being so, it provides for two main kinds of Adoptionism to have become established: in effect, one which posits the turning of God into man, and the other which transforms man into God. This Adoptionist argument posits the case that any person, by virtue of their extreme piety, may be 'adopted' as sufficiently holy as to become of divine nature. Adoptionism of any kind is—or was—regarded as heresy on the grounds that it blurs the two natures, tending for them to become fused rather than remaining separate. Jesus—generally assumed to be the Luke Jesus, as argued later—was 'made of a woman' (Galatians 4:4), whereas Christ 'was the Son of the living God' (Matthew 16:16).

During the early centuries, when Christian faiths were being settled on, there was much debate about what was heretical and what was not. Those who believed that Christ was either wholly divine or wholly human were known as Monophysites, of which there are two categories. The Docetic Monophysites maintained that Christ only *seemed* to have a human body and to suffer and die on the cross, but in reality he was wholly and solely divine. What 'body' he had was not of physical-material substance, but ethereal and phantom-like. It is common to quote II John 1:7 to nail this particular heresy: 'For many deceivers are entered into the world, who confess not that Jesus Christ is come in the flesh. This is a deceiver and antichrist.' By contrast, the Ebionic Monophysites claimed that Jesus was wholly and solely human, and did not in any way consist of a truly divine nature, and they disclaimed anything extraordinary in his conception and birth. Moreover, being mostly Jews, they believed that Christians should follow the law of Moses. Eventually, however, both kinds of Monophysitism were condemned as heresy by the early Church.

The distinguishing feature of one kind of Adoptionism that grew out of the Ebionic brand of Monophysitism was based on the belief that if a person conducted himself strictly according to God's (Mosaic) law and thereby attained perfection, that individual was worthy of 'adoption' by God and thus qualified as a *Son of God*. The apostle Peter proclaimed (II, 1:3,4) that through the Lord's divine power 'ye might be partakers of the divine nature, having escaped the corruption that is in the world through lust' (*epithumia*—inordinate desire), and the 'pollutions of the world' (II Peter, 2:20). This attitude is redolent of the ascetic practices of the Essenes, who also insisted on strict cleanliness of body, soul and spirit, which is echoed to this day in all kinds of monastic practices. By long tradition among the esoteric pre-Christian movements such as the Essenes this 'ascent' was accomplished by the successful completion of 42 stages, which are represented by the 42 'ancestors' of Christ Jesus listed in Matthew's genealogy. A physical body must needs be perfect if it were to be the vehicle for the divine Christ Being during his short sojourn on earth.

A typical exponent of this kind of Adoptionism was Paul of Samosata, Bishop of Antioch, in the third century: 'Jesus was a mortal man whose eminent virtue made him the chosen son of God.' Jesus of Nazareth was regarded as such an individual, and was therefore accorded the appropriate title. This view, however, could not be tolerated by the early Church because it disclaimed any divine involvement, and was condemned as heresy accordingly. There was the implication, too, that a purely human being could progress to divine status by dint of attaining the ultimate goal of utter perfection by his own efforts. A kind of proof-text for this viewpoint is echoed in Philippians 2:12–13: '. . . work out your own salvation with fear and trembling, for it is God who worketh in you . . .' This notion, however, could not be allowed to endure in case it corrupted the simply faithful. Nowadays there seems to be a return to this way of thinking, though very much tainted by humanistic ideas. Moreover, the strict discipline required to meet the necessary demands of a rigorous meditative life, and that of maintaining the essentially high moral standards required to attain such a level of perfection, is so daunting as to attract comparatively few aspirants.

Another kind of Adoptionism concerns those who believe that Jesus of Nazareth was purely human until his baptism in the River Jordan by John the Baptist, when the Christ Being 'descended' into his bodily vehicle and indwelt it until his death on the cross. The Synoptic Gospels (Matthew 3:17; Mark 1:11; Luke 3:22) all employ similar wording: 'This is (Thou art) my beloved Son, in whom I am well pleased.' John's description (1:32–4) reads: 'And John bare record, saying, I saw the Spirit descending from heaven like a dove, and it abode upon him . . . And I saw, and bare record that this is the Son of God.'

Moreover, it is perhaps not well enough known that certain versions of Luke read: 'This is my beloved Son. This day have

I begotten him.' The proof-text for the baptism appears in Psalm 2:7; and a very similar formula is to be seen at Acts 13:33 and Hebrews 1:5 and 5:5. Bearing in mind that Luke wrote Acts in addition to his own Gospel, this would suggest that the version appearing in most Bibles has been modified to conform with that in Matthew and Mark. Apart from these references, there is ample evidence that the person who emerged from his baptism in the River Jordan was a very different individual from the one who underwent it. Hebrews 10:5 proclaims: 'a body hast thou prepared for me (or, thou hast fitted me)'; and in Colossians 2:9–10 we read: 'For in him dwelleth all the fulness of the Godhead bodily. And ye are complete in him, which is head of all *principality* and *power*.' This is a direct reference to Christ as being a member of the exalted beings of the spiritual Hierarchies known as *Exousiai*, (rendered by most translators as Authorities or Powers), and this alone should be sufficient to discredit any notion that Christ Jesus was no more than a 'perfect human being'.

Modern orthodox Christian thinking, at least as far as the Western Churches, both Roman Catholic and Protestant, are concerned, maintain as one of the cornerstones of their faith the belief that the Christ (*ho Christos*) was 'conceived' simultaneously with—or as—Jesus in Mary's womb by supernormal means, namely, by the agency of the 'Holy Spirit'. In other words, the Incarnation of Christ is deemed to have taken place at this time: he was 'made flesh', was born of the Virgin Mary, and thereby made man in Jesus. It is fair to say that Christians of whatever denomination find the whole question of the Incarnation one of the most difficult items of faith to come to terms with, and this is complicated by the highly controversial problems associated with the 'virgin birth' or, more properly, the 'virginal conception'.

At John 1:3 we read that all things were made by him (the Creative Word) and 'without him was not any thing made that was made'. God is a spirit, and being made in his image we ourselves must also be primarily spiritual in nature, and only secondarily earthly beings, for in principle like can only produce like. We are indeed the offspring and 'children' of God, and the Christ as 'firstborn among many brethren' (Romans 8:29) was fundamentally similar to ourselves during his period of incarnation. He possessed a threefold nature whilst on earth, that is to say Spirit, Soul and Body, as do we all. This notion was succinctly put by St Leo I (440–61), often referred to as 'the one great theologian among the popes', thus: 'Being invisible in his own nature, he became visible in ours.'

Trinities divine and human

If man was made in the image of God, and if God is conceived as being threefold in nature, it would follow that man's nature is also threefold in constitution. This being so, then the 'works' of man in the world and society could be expected to reflect this threefoldness, and this is indeed the case. The doctrine of the Trinity or tri-unity of God posits a Godhead that is at once one and three. There is no doubt that the Old Testament consistently maintains that God is a unity: 'Hear, O Israel: The Lord our God is one Lord' (Deuteronomy 6:4). As following a strictly monotheistic religion, the Hebrews were conspicuous in a world in which polytheistic religious systems abounded. Indications suggesting a threefold God-head are, however, to be found in Matthew 28:19 with Jesus saying: 'Go forth therefore and make all nations my disciples; baptize men everywhere in the name of the Father and the

Son and the Holy Spirit.' Similarly, Paul writes in II Corinthians 13:14: 'The grace of the Lord Jesus Christ and the love of God and the fellowship of the Holy Spirit be with you all.' Bearing in mind that neither the word 'Trinity' nor the explicit doctrine as such appears in the Bible, it is not surprising that later disciplines within Christendom, notably various Protestant factions, contended that the tradition is unimportant anyway, asserting that it is 'unscriptural' or irrational, or even unnecessary.

Certainly, the notion of the Trinity was conceived as a mystery from the very start, and not much progress has since been made by the Churches in expounding it. Small wonder therefore that the Holy Spirit largely became to be regarded as a vaguely inspirational abstraction, and the Son as not so much the Christ, the Messiah of exalted origins, but rather a simple carpenter with outstanding charismatic qualities. Oddly enough, nowadays not much reference seems to be made to the fact that Jesus of Nazareth was, whatever else, a highly educated rabbi who, even when a mere boy of twelve years old, could hold his own in debate with learned scholars (Luke 2:46–7). His conversation with Nathaniel *the Israelite*—an appellation which reveals that Nathaniel was an initiate of the fifth order, namely, *Spirit of the People*—is reported in John's Gospel (1:45–51). A further implication that Nathaniel was a man of some importance is confirmed by his presence with several other disciples at a significant post-resurrection gathering (John 21:2).

With the advent of the Christ, the Messiah, as 'God's only Son', the early Christians were faced with the problem of having to deny the tenet steadfastly held by the Jews that God is One and indivisible. They were faced with the difficulties of explaining how One can be Three and the Three can be One.

By recognizing the Christ Being who indwelt Jesus of Nazareth as the Son of God, the early Christians found themselves in disagreement with the orthodox Jews, who held that the Eternal could have no sons. Furthermore, they were obliged to stress that Christ was the *only* Son of God in order to avoid accusations of polytheism. With due recognition of the Holy Spirit, however, a satisfactory concept of the essential Trinity—the One in Three and the Three in One— was arrived at.

Needless to say, controversies abounded at the time, but they crystallized into two main tendencies: (a) distinctness among the Three, but at the cost of their equality and hence of their unity (Subordinationism); and (b) emphasis on the unity of the Three, but at the cost of their distinction as 'persons' (Modalism). A further bone of contention was that of the so-called 'procession' issue: does the Holy Spirit proceed from the Son, or from Father and Son both? In the very early centuries the tendency was very strong to subordinate the Holy Spirit to the Son, who, not surprisingly, was regarded as subordinate to the Father. John's Gospel (14:26) has Jesus saying to his disciples: 'But the Comforter, which is the Holy Spirit, whom the Father will send in my name . . .' Similarly, in 15:26 we read: 'But when the Comforter is come, whom I will send unto you from the Father, even the Spirit of truth, which proceedeth from the Father, he shall testify of me . . .' The whole matter is obscure, and it is not surprising that it was commonly seen fit to let the whole affair remain a mystery.

In pre-Christian times the individual person was regarded primarily as a unity; both the Hebrews and the Egyptians regarded the human being not so much as a body with a soul-spiritual nature or a soul-spiritual being with a bodily nature, but as a whole, an indissoluble unity. This notion of oneness is reflected in the Hebrew belief of one God. It is not surprising, therefore, that the notion of the Trinity and of the human being as comprising spirit, soul and body emerged at the same time. Irenaeus (*c.* 130–*c.* 200) also propounded it in his treatise *Against Heresies*, which is worth quoting:

> The perfect person consists of these three: flesh, soul and spirit. One of them saves and fashions—that is, the spirit. Another is united and formed—that is, the flesh; while that which lies between the two is the soul, which sometimes follows the spirit and is raised by it, but at other times sympathizes with the flesh and is drawn into it by earthly passions.

The time was to come, however, when succeeding Ecumenical Councils laid more emphasis on mankind as beings of body and soul only, thus paving the way for the dualistic concept of the human being which flourished increasingly thereafter. Nowadays, psychologists have succeeded in banishing the soul, so that we are left with a perfectly monistic conception of the human being endorsed by modern science, namely, as consisting of body only.

In everyday speech, distinctions between soul and spirit are not always made, the two terms being used interchangeably. People often speak of mind and spirit, or even mind and soul, and seem to make little differentiation between the two. This is understandable enough; but it helps to distinguish between soul and spirit if we think of these two principles as being the bases for our faculties of feeling and thinking respectively. 'Mind' is generally associated with the more intellectual of mental activities. This seems to be instinctively felt by many people who employ the word 'soul' to refer to the emotional life, and 'spirit' to the entity that is regarded as responsible for our 'higher' thoughts, ideals, moral attributes and suchlike. Now we all know that our thoughts and feelings influence one another, but we moreover realize, on reflection, that most of these have their origin in bodily sensations. In other words, it is our senses which provide the basis for so much of our feeling—and thinking also, for that matter. Furthermore, it is common experience that it is easier for most of us to find feelings for our reasons than reasons for our feelings.

Evolution betokens reincarnation

It is generally understood that God is absolute and change-less, whereas his Creation, including humanity, is subject to ceaseless change, and hence evolution, made manifest in processes of continuous metamorphosis. This means that the human ego, enshrined in the spirit, thereby possesses endless possibility for advancement. For this to come about, how-ever, necessarily involves the notion of reincarnation, re-peated earthly lives, and this is precisely what Origen (185–254) taught. He could see, as increasing numbers of people today can see, that a single earthly life, one incarnation only, limited as it necessarily is in so many ways and circumstances that constrict and constrain, from socio-economic factors to disability, disease and possible early death, offers ridiculously few possibilities for advancement.

But to return to the rather simplistic notion of man pre-valent among early Christians as a being of body and soul, or body and spirit. This was probably based on the notion of Christ Jesus possessing a twofold nature—a heavenly and an earthly, expressed as soul and body respectively. How these two principles were arranged in respect of each other was a matter of endless debate during those early years. Various theories concerning such matters, tortuously argued about but never resolved, concerned such analogies as mixture, predominance, union, association, juxtaposition, composition, mutual contact and, needless to say, confusion (*sic*). The Church Fathers, understandably enough from a limited point of view, believed that the soul or spiritual part of a human being emanated from God, the physical-material part obviously originating in the natural parents.

The unsophisticated approach of those early thinkers could get no further than a dualistic belief that human beings are constituted of body and soul only, with the personality residing in the soul. They had, if at all, only a hazy idea of what is designated *passim* as the 'ego', which is that principle that imparts a strong, unmistakable sense of self in its activity of coordinating and unifying everything we experience throughout our individual lives, and is capable of growth and development whilst drawing on the faculty of memory which serves it.

Other disputes and controversies

It is difficult to discuss the nature of the Christ without referring to some of the more important figures and controversies that surround this mystery. There were others besides those briefly discussed elsewhere, but perhaps the most important among these is the so-called Arian controversy centred on the Greek theologian Arius (d. AD 336), which lasted for more than 60 years. He contended that the Logos, as the Word and therefore the agent of Creation, must have been more than man. As the Creator of all other beings he could justifiably be called God. Christ, however, in view of his status as the Son of God, must be regarded as being inferior to the Father. The crux of the matter centred on the term *homoousion* (of one substance or essence). This is not a scriptural term, however, and objections were made to the effect that Jesus Christ was indeed God, but that Arius was guilty of regarding him as a creature of God. A compromise suggested by some Arians was to substitute the term *homoiousion* (of like essence). A Council was called at Nicaea in 325, with the result that Arianism was formally repudiated and a creed adopted that distinctly affirmed what Arius had denied. He was banished by imperial decree, and the so-called Nicene Creed was formally adopted and widely accepted in the West, though many Eastern Churches were reluctant to adopt it. The danger of the idea coming about that Christ would eventually be regarded as no more than a mere man was thus avoided, though it must be reiterated at this point that, as mentioned elsewhere, this state of affairs is very widespread in modern times.

Another heresy in the eyes of the early Church was enshrined in the teachings of Apollinarius, who was born in Laodicea in 318, of which he was appointed bishop in 362. The arguments centred on Arianism were still reverberating around Christendom at that time. Whereas Arius had emphasized rather the subordination of, and the human nature of, the Son, Apollinarius taught that Christ was only one person, and was identifiable with the Logos, the Son. Based on this assertion, his contention was that, since the Logos was not subject to change (and in this he was in direct opposition to Arius), and since the human being comprises body, soul and spirit, the place of this latter highest principle of Jesus of Nazareth must have been taken by the Logos or Christ. The view of the orthodox Church was that if the Spirit of Jesus was thus displaced, the Incarnation must be deemed to be incomplete in all respects, with the inevitable implication that Jesus Christ could not be regarded as perfect God and perfect man. The proposition underlying this conclusion was that what the Logos did not assume he could not redeem. In other words, if Christ had not assumed the whole of Jesus of Nazareth's personality, which in the belief of the Church was identifiable with the spirit (*nous*), there would remain in the human constitution something that was not changed and that therefore could not be redeemed. At the Second Ecumenical Council held at Constantinople in 381, however, Apollinarianism was condemned.

We can already discern the elements of Adoptionist thinking which was inevitably to follow. Diodore (Bishop of Tarsus 378–94) taught that the Son of God is to be distinguished from the son of David. The latter was simply the temple for the indwelling of the Word or Logos. Now one of Diodore's pupils was Theodore of Mopsuestia (*c.* 350–428), one of whose pupils was Nestorius, after whom the Adoptionist heresy of these two theologians known as Nestorianism was named. Theodore, therefore, was a Nestorian before Nestorius, and he pointed out that three methods of union between the Son of God (the Christ or Logos) and the son of David (Jesus of Nazareth) were possible: (1) the assumption of the manhood by the Logos; (2) the cohesion of the two natures; and (3) the indwelling of the Logos in the manhood. The last notion was the one that seemed the most likely to Theodore, and so he upheld the notion of Adoptionism.

Nestorius was Patriarch of Constantinople (428–31), an eloquent speaker and zealous for what in his mind was orthodoxy. He could not subscribe to the notion that divinity and humanity could be united in a single self-conscious personality. He was particularly opposed to Apollinarius, arguing that since the Logos was not subject to change Christ could have had no human will, and that since man is divided into body and soul the personality must be identified with the soul. Therefore, as far as the nature of Christ was concerned, the human soul must have been replaced by the Logos. All this demonstrates the muddled thinking that was going on during the fourth and fifth centuries, simply because of the bizarre assumption that Christ Jesus, not Jesus only, was conceived by Mary as a result of divine intervention in the shape of the Holy Spirit.

The upshot of all the wranglings that went on was the calling of a General Council by Emperor Theodosius II to meet at Ephesus in 431 in order to settle the controversy. Nestorius was reluctant to go, scornfully asserting that it was impossible to call Mary *Theotokos* (Mother of God) because it was not possible that God should be born of woman, and that it was clearly ridiculous for a child of two or three to be called God. Such assertions angered the Church authorities in both Rome and Alexandria, where there seemed to be strong allegiance to Mary as 'mother of God'. Nestorius and his party of bishops were late in arriving at the Council, only to find that his ideas had already been condemned. He died in 439 during banishment to upper Egypt after much hardship and suffering. The Nestorian party, however, did not accept the decision of the Council, with the result that Nestorianism has survived in certain factions of the Eastern Church to this day.

Although both factions accepted the Nicene Creed, there were fundamental differences between the Eastern Churches centred on Antioch and the Western Churches influenced by the Alexandrian school. In Antioch they approached the mystery of the Word made flesh from the human side, trying to show how the man Christ Jesus was truly Son of God. In Alexandria they started with the recognition of Christ's eternal Godhead and proceeded to show how he was truly man. But both can be seen to be falling between two stools because of faulty assumptions or premises. The two points of view could be reconciled if Christ were not regarded as being conceived in Mary by the Holy Spirit, the resulting child already being deemed to comprise the two natures, divine and human. The Luke Mary, as maintained throughout, was the mother of Jesus of Nazareth only, the latter becoming the vehicle for the Christ Being only on the occasion of his baptism in the River Jordan. The Incarnation took place at that time, and not at the time of conception. Jesus of Nazareth had a natural mother, and therefore the Christ can never at any time be said to have been *born*. One often hears the expression 'Christ-child', a thoughtless as well as perilous mistake, since the Christ Being, as a leading member of the exalted spiritual Hierarchy of *Exousiai*, or Spirits of Form, never had a childhood (this issue is fully discussed in Chapter 6).

Some modern points of view

Common sense would suggest that, as there was only one Christ, there could have been only one Jesus of Nazareth. Both Mark and Luke speak of 'Jesus Christ', though it is noteworthy that Matthew calls particular attention to Jesus' Messiahship. In 1:16 he writes '... Mary, of whom *was* born Jesus who *is* called Christ', and this gives a clue to the 'generation' from Jesus the man to the Christ which he later became. Matthew (1:17) leaves no room for doubt by stating that 'from the carrying away into Babylon *to the Christ* are fourteen generations'. This phrase is translated as 'unto Christ' (Authorized Version), thus omitting the all-significant definite article, and 'unto the Messiah' (New English Bible), in which it is included, as it should be. Now if the generations are counted in the usual way, there are only 13 generations, not 14 as the genealogical listing shows.

Pontius Pilate, when he delivered Jesus Christ to the chief priests for crucifixion, said: '*Ecce homo*'—'Behold the man' (John 19:5). To him he was merely a man, a nuisance and a source of turmoil in the Jewish community. As far as Pilate was concerned, his prisoner was Jesus of Nazareth, the King of the Jews and nothing more than an ordinary human being. During the last few centuries there has been steady and consistent drift towards the same notion that Christ was a man, and a man only. In other words the *name* 'Jesus' has become inextricably identified with the *title* 'Christ'. It is commonly thought—and even emphasized by modern-day clerics—that Jesus Christ was a name comprising first or given name and surname that customarily we all bear. Such a belief cannot be reconciled with John 8:58: Jesus said unto them, 'Verily, verily I say unto you, Before Abraham was, I am,' and similar statements appear at Isaiah 43:13, John 1:1, 17:5, 24, and Colossians 1:17.

Only the closest followers of Christ Jesus knew that he was in fact the Messiah; as far as they were concerned he was the Son of God, and they accepted this as a simple fact. The development of any kind of systematic Christology had to wait for Paul; and as mentioned elsewhere, it is highly significant that, at the time of his Damascus experience, he recognized the risen Christ as having indwelt Jesus of Nazareth. The disciples, however, acknowledged this after the baptism in the Jordan, whilst Jesus was still alive. The claims with regard to Adoptionism as argued and demonstrated all along are thus seen to be verified.

In the early years of the Church there were, as there are now, people who looked upon Jesus the Christ as a mere man, whose nature was as other men, namely, human. Then, perhaps, he was accorded more respect and regard than he is now, when he is widely regarded as 'the simple man of Nazareth, who went about doing good'. One church poster which read 'Carpenter from Nazareth seeking joiners' is indicative of how matey and familiar such attitudes have become. One would hardly expect the writers of such an appeal to genuflect in the direction of any altar; and one can well imagine Nestorius snorting: 'What! do you think I would pray to a mere carpenter?'

There is agreement, however, in so far as Jesus Christ—or more properly Jesus *the* Christ—comprised both divine and human natures, whether these operated separately or not, a matter which occupied the Church Fathers to an inordinate extent. Nowadays people do not seem to be concerned with this problem; but it is a problem, and a growing one, for it seems to be at the root of a new kind of Adoptionism, or rather a revival of an old form of it which was declared heretical by the early Church. A particularly crude example of this trend appears in a fairly recent book (*Know your Faith in a Decade of Evangelism*) by British cleric John Young: 'At first (Christ) was a title: Jesus *the* Christ. But because the title belonged so closely to the person, it became part of his name. Hence Jesus Christ. Just as John the Blacksmith at some point became John Smith.'

A further step along this particular road to the new humanism was taken by the same author: 'On ascending into heaven, Jesus did not shed his humanity. He took it with him. It is not an angel who sits at the Father's right hand: it is a human being.' Lowering Christ to the status of angel is questionable enough, but inferring that he was a human being, albeit not quite like the rest of us, is even more flagrant. In his letter to the Colossians (2:18), Paul scorns those 'who go in for self-mortification and angel-worship'. Furthermore, the writer of the letter to the Hebrews states quite clearly (1:4–6) that Christ 'took his seat at the right hand of Majesty on high, raised far above the angels, as the title he has inherited is far superior to theirs. God never said to any angel, 'Thou art my Son; this day have I begotten thee,' or again, 'I will be father to him, and he shall be to me a Son.' (Incidentally, Dr George Carey, a former Archbishop of Canterbury, was 'delighted to commend' Mr Young's book.)

It is fair to say that in our highly materialistic and intellectual age, with its emphasis on proof of a scientific nature, knowledge of spiritual matters barely exists. Ask anyone what they understand by the nature of the Christ, and the probable answer, if given, will get no further than the 'Son of God' routine. Biblical scholars may have a fine time discussing Christ as the Logos, his pre-existence and suchlike; but these important matters scarcely concern most Christians, whose bookshelves are unlikely to bear straightforward biblical commentaries, not to mention Greek texts.

The belief of the pre-existence of the Messiah was widespread among the Jews of pre-Christian times. 'Wisdom' also means 'law' in rabbinic literature, and it is easy to see the connection between these two concepts in scientific terms. 'Before the sun and signs were created, before the stars and the heaven were made, his name (Messiah) was named before the Lord of Spirits' runs Enoch 48:3. To follow up an already familiar theme, 'he hath been chosen and hidden before him, before the creation of the world', as it states in Enoch 48:6. The belief that both the Messiah and Wisdom were actually created as incorporeal beings before the creation of the world was strong, and even nowadays Jews look upon Wisdom and the Messiah as two separate beings, the former to be revealed through Moses and latter the pre-existent Redeemer to be born of the House of David.

Paul goes as far as identifying these two, describing Christ as 'the power of God and the wisdom of God' (I Cor. 1:24; I Cor. 2:7). He was probably drawing on his obviously wide knowledge of the Wisdom literature, but which has been confirmed by his direct if supersensibly gained knowledge of the Christ. Of the many attributes attaching to the term *Logos*, wisdom is a well-respected one. Wisdom is that 'which pervades and penetrates all things' (Wisdom of Solomon 7:24) and 'administers all things' (Wisdom 8:1), where also the Spirit of the Lord is identified with wisdom, which 'holdeth all things together' (Wisdom 1:7). In this connection Paul says of the pre-existent Christ that 'in him all things hold together' (Colossians 1:17), which is also confirmed by the Jewish author of the Epistle to the Hebrews (1:3).

Eventually, the inevitable will happen, namely, that when the experimenters and researchers have stripped off the last veil wisdom will be theirs; they will encounter the Word, the Logos, Christ himself. In their zeal and dedication in the pursuit of satisfying the unquenchable urge innate in all human beings to *know*, this is bound to happen. The Church Fathers were close to regarding wisdom as an entity with almost a life of its own, some going as far as to personify it and identify it with the Logos. However, wisdom is one thing, but knowledge quite another. No one would deny that the cosmos, and the necessary order that this by definition implies, is the manifestation of the wisdom inherent in it and integral to it. This very fact facilitates all the discoveries of science, which are wonderful only on account of the inbuilt wisdom that is literally dis-covered and made apparent thereby. One day the boundary limiting the visible and material will be crossed, and the invisible and immaterial encountered; scientists will then discover that they have crossed the threshold from the world of matter into the world of spirit. There, what will they find other than the Logos?

John, Luke and Paul—Adoptionists all

It is clear from the (alternative) statement in Luke's Gospel (3:22), 'Thou art my beloved Son; this day have I begotten thee,' concerning the Sonship of Christ Jesus that he was a convinced Adoptionist, as was his associate Paul. The latter takes matters further, for at Romans 1:3–4 we read: 'Concerning his (God's) Son Jesus Christ our Lord, which was made of the seed of David according to the flesh; and declared to be the Son of God in power, according to the spirit of holiness, by the resurrection from the dead.' It is clear from this that Paul had no conception of anything other than a normal birth for 'Jesus', and there is nothing to deny that this statement is applicable to both the Matthew Jesus and the Luke Jesus. It is clear from this that Paul had no conception of anything other than a normal birth, and there is nothing to deny that this statement is applicable to both the Matthew Jesus and the Luke Jesus. It is significant that David is the safe and convenient benchmark ancestor to which all kinds of references can be made. From David sprang both lines of descent culminating at the two births—that is to say, the kingly line from Solomon and the priestly line from Nathan, of which more later.

Having determined the physical origins of Christ Jesus, Paul sets out the criterion for stating that he was God's Son also, and this is dependent on the fact that he had risen from the dead or resurrected. It is this fact that gives proof of his divine origins, and hence his Sonship. This obviously negates the mistaken idea that the Christ was 'born', that the Incarnation took place at the birth of Jesus, and then only. But it was his baptism in the River Jordan that marked his divine Sonship, and hence his 'birth'. Confirmation of this involves the resurrection event. It was patently clear to all that the 'person' who was resurrected was the same one that was crucified; this 'individual' was the same one who was baptized by John, and this man was Jesus of Nazareth. This person's identity was confirmed at the time of the Temple event and in Luke's genealogy. Evidence has already been offered that the boy who sat among the doctors was the Luke Jesus, into whom the individuality of the Matthew Jesus had entered.

Rudolf Steiner asserted that the process of incarnation of the Christ Being into Jesus of Nazareth was gradual, lasting for the whole of the 40 days he spent undergoing the temptations in the wilderness after his baptism by John. It is reported by Matthew (4:1–11) and Luke (4:1–13), both in close agreement. The now fully established Christ Jesus had become duly qualified to realize his mission, and to announce in the synagogue that the prophecy of Isaiah at 61:1,2 was commencing its fulfilment (Luke 4:16–21). His hearers in the synagogue found it difficult to grasp the actuality that he was very different from the Jesus they had known as Joseph the carpenter's son of little significance, yet who was now 'speaking the words of God' (John 3:34–6).

It is no coincidence that when 'Jesus' is mentioned by orthodox theologians and religionists it is the Luke Jesus they are referring to. It is during the temple event that this Jesus, then a boy of twelve, declared, 'wist ye not that I must be about my Father's business?' It is only after his baptism by John, when the Sonship of Jesus of Nazareth was confirmed (Luke 3:22), that Luke was, immediately after this event, justified in tracing the boy's genealogy right back to Abraham, Adam, and thence to God (Luke 3:38). This verse refers to Adam as his son, which applies also to the boy of twelve by virtue of descent. These circumstances, taken together and in sequence, clearly show the soundness and validity of the Adoptionist view that the Incarnation occurred at the baptism of Jesus of Nazareth, *and not at his birth.*

As if in order to accentuate this very fact, Isaiah (1:3) mentions the cow and the donkey (ox and ass) as 'knowing their master' (whereas Israel does not). Demetrius of Antioch, in a discourse, attributes to Salome (she who was a close follower of the Messiah) immediate recognition of Joseph, the husband of Mary, asking him to find a midwife. 'By the time Joseph and Salome had returned to the caravanserai the child had been born. When they entered the house they saw the child in a manger, and *the ox and the ass* protecting him.' Ancient tradition maintains that this reference to these particular creatures, which are often to be seen on Christmas card reproductions of ancient paintings, was an attempt to prove that Jesus was born naturally; that is to say, by vaginal expulsion between the urethra and the anus—representative of the ox and the ass. For most Christmas card buyers the presence of such humble creatures is taken for granted, but such an arrangement also lends weight to the claims of Adoptionists.

Thus the purely human nature of him who was known as Jesus of Nazareth is established beyond all doubt. The divine nature which, in the shape of the Logos, 'descended' into him was, it must be argued, at the time of the baptism in the Jordan. This neat Adoptionist notion was favoured by many Gnostics, although denied by some early Church Fathers. They were convinced that Jesus—and the one and only Jesus, of course—was a 'mixture', a technical term of the philosophers of the time, characterized by Philo as a 'mutual co-extension of dissimilar parts entering into one another at all points, while the various qualities can still be distinguished...' Hence the coexistence of the two natures—human and divine—was considered to be perfectly feasible and possible.

Matthew, Mark, some versions of Luke, and John merely confirm that Christ was indeed the only Son of God, in whom he was well pleased, on whom his favour rests and so on. In the view of the majority, therefore, the versions of Luke which make clear inferences to the birth of the Christ, *as a heavenly being with no earthly body of his own*, at the baptism in the Jordan were largely disregarded. There is also the matter of the proof-text in Psalm 2:7, 'I will declare a decree: The Lord hath said unto me, Thou art my Son; this day have I begotten thee,' which seems uncomfortably convenient; the idea of such an exalted spiritual being designated the Son of God descending into an earthly body may have been too drastic for early—and some contemporary—theologians to accept. The preferred belief is that Jesus of Nazareth as the Christ was born of the (Luke) Virgin Mary by virginal conception in Bethlehem, and that his baptism merely marked his 'Epiphany' or manifestation to everyone, serving as a kind of authentication that here was indeed the long-awaited Messiah.

Generations of biblical scholars have wondered why the birth stories are there at all; but their blatant contradictions in themselves may have served as a deliberate pointer to the true facts. Jesus of Nazareth does not become 'the Christ' until the event of the baptism in the Jordan. Only then does Jesus become the 'Son of God' (Matthew 3:17; Mark 1:11; Luke 3:22; John 1:34). In John 1:41 Andrew finds his brother Simon and tells him: 'We have found the Messiah, which is, being interpreted, Christ.' Later, at Sychar's well, Jesus reveals his Messianic identity to the Samaritan woman. John also reports lively discussion among the people of Jerusalem as to whether Jesus was in very fact the Christ (7:25–52), and his life was threatened on more than one occasion (9:59; 10:31).

Eventually, of course, recognition came; Jesus of Nazareth was deemed to have been filled entirely with the Holy Spirit, and could claim Sonship on account of his heavenly birth as well as his earthly birth. Paul describes, I Corinthians 15:8, how Christ appeared to him last of all, as unto one born out of due time. As a Jew, he was well acquainted with the idea of the coming Messiah, but as Saul he could not accept that Jesus was the Christ-bearer. He actively concerned himself with opposing this, and it is one of the most dramatic and remarkable facts in the history of Christendom how Paul, on the road to Damascus, became aware that Jesus of Nazareth had indeed been indwelt by the Christ. He had never known Christ Jesus in life, as had the disciples, yet Paul knew the Christ as a discarnate being after his death and resurrection.

In I Corinthians 15:45–9 we read of Christ as the last or 'second Adam' (see also verse 22), and as Luke was known to have been a pupil of Paul (and author of the Acts of the Apostles), one is not surprised to find Luke's genealogical table leading from the 'last Adam' to the 'first Adam'. The placing of the table by Luke immediately after the baptism in the River Jordan is highly significant. Interesting too is the commentary St Jerome gave on Isaiah 11:2: 'And the spirit of the Lord shall rest upon him, the spirit of wisdom and understanding, the spirit of knowledge and the fear of the Lord.' He wrote: 'The spirit of the Lord shall rest upon him not partially as in the case of other holy men; but, according to the Gospel written in the Hebrew speech, which the Nazarenes read: "There shall descend upon him the whole fount of the Holy Spirit . . ."' In the Gospel of the Hebrews is written: 'And it came to pass when the Lord was come up out of the water, the whole fount of the Holy Spirit descended and rested upon him: My son, in all the prophets was I waiting for thee that thou shouldst come, and I might rest in thee. For thou are my rest, thou art my first begotten Son, that reignest for ever.'

Christ and the Sun

The modern mind does not find it easy to cope with expressions such as Clement of Alexandria employs when referring to Christ as the 'Sun of the Resurrection, begotten before the morning star, giving life with thy rays'. Now this kind of language is that of the mystic rather than the rational thinker, and the result of pictorial imagery rather than reasoned argument. Such pictorial language as the Church Fathers employed to express their ideas is often looked upon in modern times, not as representative of reality, but as mere metaphor, personification and other figurative linguistic devices.

It is of very great significance that belief in the pagan gods faded rapidly during the first three centuries of our era, for the rise of a highly sophisticated religion such as Christianity, based as it was on the history of the Hebraic peoples with its long tradition of prophecy and spiritual development, was inexorable by reason of its authenticity and power. The scriptures of the Israelites sparkle and flash with innumerable references to a coming Saviour or Messiah whose mission was not only of consequence to the chosen people, but also to the whole human race. The historical reality, namely, the fact that all the early Christians were Jews, and the modern scene wherein Jews are clearly recognizable by their very reversal of this position, is at once remarkable and enigmatic.

Everyone knows of the so-called Twelve Days of Christmas, which span from the night of 24/25 December until 6 January. According to popular belief concerning the nativity of Jesus Christ (rather than just plain Jesus of Nazareth), 25 December was the date when the shepherds attended the newborn baby, and 6 January was when the Magi visited to pay their respects. Such dates were settled on for other reasons, as discussed elsewhere, and are far from being factual. From that notion it would have been a short step to associate one story with Luke and the other with Matthew, but no one dared to suggest that there were actually two births, even though the New Testament says so.

It was St Jerome (c. 347–420), whose Vulgate was the first authentic Latin translation of the Bible from the Hebrew, who popularized the date of 25 December as that for celebrating the birth of Christ, and the confusion of this with 6 January is a result of the changes in thinking and conceptualization that went on at around this time. The date of 24 December was traditionally the day dedicated to Adam and Eve, and here may be discerned a possible connection in the minds of the early Christians with the birth of the second Adam.

Teachings that leaked from the Mystery Centres and other esoteric orders, which guarded their secrets closely (allowing only those who were initiated access to them), indicated that the Creator of the world itself dwelt on the sun. This Being was destined to descend to the earth to impart the necessary impetus to enable man to be restored to his original divine state that had existed prior to his Fall, and was none other than the exalted spiritual Being known as the Christ. Certainly, there is much to connect Christ with the sun. In Malachi 4:1 he is referred to as 'the Sun of Righteousness', in typical mystical style. Modern scholars find it difficult to understand why the early Church Fathers spoke in praise of Christ the sun, and of the Church itself as a kind of spiritual moon. Later on, the Virgin Mary herself was identified with the moon, but the whole theology of those early years was heavy with symbol, and metaphorical allusions can hardly be claimed to be without some substance in reality.

The sun is the source of light, whether direct or derived sources such as wood, coal, crude oil, natural gas and suchlike, and it is not for nothing that John (1:9) refers to Christ as being 'the true light which enlightens everyone that comes into the world'. Small wonder, therefore, that Christ was referred to in terms of the sun to the extent of being identified with it. It is not without significance, either, that the date settled on for the birth of Jesus of Nazareth was that which approximated to the winter solstice, when the days were shortest and the nights longest, namely, 24 December. This day was the eighth day before the Calends (the 1st) of January, when the Romans celebrated the feast of Saturnalia, the Egyptians Cronia, and the Alexandrians Cicellia. Thereafter the days begin to lengthen, and the power of the sun to increase accordingly, and these facts were not lost on the early Christians, well inured to the rich diet of symbol upon which religious thinkers relied.

It needs scarcely be pointed out that the sun, which together with the earth was regarded as the giver of all life, was closely observed in its apparent behaviour throughout the year and its important connections with the seasons. The sun-orb, being observed to get weaker and weaker during the winter months, was thought to have died, and the priest-king, as 'sun' of many a primitive tribe was obliged to be (lightly) buried in the earth at the time of the winter solstice, there to remain for three days before his 'resurrection' was effected.

The Roman cult of the Sol Invictus, the Invincible Sun, upheld the notion of a sun god that epitomized the virtues of all other gods, and in AD 321 Constantine decreed that the official day of rest should be Sunday rather than Saturday, the traditional Hebrew Sabbath Day. Until then, the official birthday of Jesus was celebrated on 6 January, but it was deemed that it should coincide with Natalis Invictus, the Birth of the Sun on 25 December. This date falls at the time of the winter solstice, when the sun is as it were reborn, when the days begin to lengthen and the power of the sun begins to strengthen. The aureole of the erstwhile sun god was, not surprisingly perhaps, adopted as the traditional halo which the Christians reserved for their holy families.

A Roman chronographer's record for AD 354 contains two notices involving the same day, namely, 25 December, which reads, '*VIII Kalendas Ianuarias Natalis Invicti,*' and '*VIII Kalendas Ianuarias natus Christus in Bethlehem Iudiae.*' This would prove that at least liturgical recognition had been made that 25 December was the day that Christ was born in

Bethlehem of Judaea, as well as the day of birth of the Invincible, that is to say reborn, sun. Significantly, therefore, we have connections between the Son of God and the sun being made quite openly. The establishment of a feast associated with the rebirth of the sun at the time of the winter solstice to coincide with the date of Christ's birth seems to be a matter of expediency on the part of those responsible for it, rather than in the interests of cold fact. But, as has been maintained all along, we do not seem to be dealing with material facts, but rather with symbolical ones. But who in the then world of conflicting ideologies and interpretations of past prophecies and current events can be identified as representing the truth?

The German scholar and Jesuit Hugo Rahner went as far as to state: 'And when at Christmas Christ is born as the true *Sol Novus* (New Sun), when in the dark of Easter Eve he arises as the true *Sol Invictus* (Unconquered Sun), there now stands beside him that exalted woman of whom in the Apocalypse is stated that she is clothed with the sun and the moon at her feet. Mary has given birth to the sun...' The affiliation between the sun as representing the Messiah and the son of Mary can easily be discerned here. The Greeks looked upon Selene, the moon, as the primal cause of all birth, and the view was common among the early Church leaders that Mary had given birth to the Sun of Righteousness in the shape of Christ. Thinking Christians will be readily forgiven for getting lost in the wealth of symbol and metaphor, for nothing seems to be stated in plain and simple language.

Rahner further quotes a Syrian writer, Bar Salibi: 'The reason why the Fathers changed this feast from 6 January to 25 December was, it is said, as follows. The heathen were accustomed on 25 December to celebrate the birthday of the sun and to light fires in honour of the day, and even Christians were invited to take part in these festivities. When the Doctors of the Church observed that Christians were being induced to participate in these practices, they decided to celebrate this day as the true anniversary of Christ's birth and to keep 6 January for the celebration of the feast of Epiphany, and this custom they have continued to observe to the present day together with the practice of the lighting of fires.'

In his *Panarion*, Epiphanius of Salamis states that Christ was born on the eighth day before the Ides of January (i.e. 13 January), or 13 days after the winter solstice, nominally 24 December and, according to modern calendars, on 6 January. He goes on to quote Ephraem, 'a wise man from among the Syrians', as saying that this had to happen 'in order that it might be a type for the number resulting when we add to our Lord Jesus Christ his twelve apostles, for it is the fulfilment of the number 13, of the 13 days since the waxing of the sun'. All this goes to show the extent to which various writers and contributors went in order to justify their ideas.

Matters of the Epiphany

It is true that the Romans celebrated the feast of Sol Invictus at the time of the winter solstice. January 6 has been determined as the date of the manifestation of the divine nature of Christ to the Gentiles as represented by the Magi, the so-called Epiphany. The connotations thickly clustered around the very word *epiphaneia* are so complex and multi-ordinate that they are difficult to unravel. Most scholars agree that the feast of Epiphany was regarded by the members of the early Church from the very beginning as a celebration of Christ's birthday, which was introduced in order to underpin the notion that Jesus Christ had been born of the Virgin Mary and that with his 'epiphany' upon the earth his mission was deemed to have begun. In language common at the time, the sun, the 'dayspring from on high', had begun to shine, bringing light, healing and grace to all mankind (Hebrews 2:14; II Timothy 1:10; I Corinthians 15:54, 55).

Furthermore, and importantly so, the word 'epiphany' signified the birthday of a god even to the Greeks and others, and by the fourth century this concept was well established, and was used interchangeably with *theophaneia* (manifestation of [a] god), and even *genethlia* (birthday). Thus 6 January became firmly established as the birthday of Jesus Christ, and 25 December was still regarded by the pagans as the time of rebirth of the sun, as marked by the winter solstice. So we have considerable confusion concerning the birth (or rebirth) of the sun as celestial body at around 24 December and the 'birth' of Christ at the Epiphany—the Christ who was widely acknowledged as the 'Sun' in numerous senses, as we have seen.

So we have the somewhat bizarre confusion between the birth (or rebirth) of the sun as celestial body on 24 December and the 'birth' of Christ at the Epiphany—the Christ who was widely acknowledged as the 'Sun' in numerous senses, as we have seen. The much respected Clement of Alexandria reported that the Gnostics regarded 6 January as the true 'birthday' of Christ, when, at the baptism in the Jordan, he was 'born' by virtue of his descent from heaven into the body of Jesus of Nazareth. It bears repetition that there is firm scriptural evidence for this, as versions of Luke 3:22 report the voice from heaven as saying, 'Thou art my beloved Son; this day have I begotten thee,' and the same words appear in Hebrews 1:5 and 5:5. Psalms 2:7 reads, 'I will declare the decree: the Lord hath said unto me, Thou art my Son; this day I have begotten thee,' which is quoted in Acts 13:33. This version seems to have been less favourable than the reports by the other evangelists to the early Church, but it can quite justifiably be seen as supporting the conviction of the Gnostics.

Moreover, this belief was firmly based on the conviction that there was only one Jesus and only one Christ with whom he was identified. It was rational to think this; it was inconceivable that there were two children called Jesus, both of whose parents were called Joseph and Mary. There was only one Epiphany at the baptism in Jordan, and only one Jesus of Nazareth who underwent it. Yet the evidence of the genealogies is overwhelming and undeniable. The problem was seemingly insoluble, and has remained so, but a solution there is bound to be.

It need scarcely be said that there are many other mysteries in the Gospels and other scriptures which would appear to demand resolution, but which have defied all attempts to achieve this. Obvious examples are the miracles, the so-called virgin birth, the Transfiguration, empty tomb, Ascension and so on—the list is endless. Such tasks have been long since abandoned by many scholars as fruitless, but this does not mean that solutions to these riddles do not exist. The case is, rather, that they have not been found, for it is inconceivable that the writers of the Scriptures would not have had reasons for relating what they did, even if they refer to experiences known only to themselves. Rudolf Steiner was able to clarify many of these enigmas from his spiritual investigations into the Akashic Records, but the contents of his lectures on the Gospels have been ignored or rejected by orthodox biblical scholars because of their highly controversial nature. The

time may come, however, when orthodox Christendom will—
perhaps in sheer desperation—come to regard the Scriptures
in the light of genuine spirituality rather than the fixed and
rigid materialistic manner which they stubbornly perpetuate,
but which is increasingly failing to satisfy the needs of the
twenty-first century and beyond.

The truth is that with all the keenness of mind, the ingen-
uity, the philological and linguistic, historical, archaeological
and other academic skills, allied to the capacity for sheer hard
and persistent effort displayed by generations of scholars,
more mysteries remain than have been satisfactorily resolved.
Why the investigations by Rudolf Steiner have not been taken
into account by orthodoxy is lamentable. It is pointless to
argue, at least at an exoteric level, about these genealogies
and their glaring irreconcilability. Steiner, however, from his
spiritual researches, was able to offer explanations that are at
once reasonable and acceptable of such incompatibilities as
well as numerous other seeming difficulties—for him there
were few.

2
THE GOSPELS: A BRIEF OVERVIEW

We are now living in a time when people must become more and more acquainted with the nature of the supersensible world, if they are to become equal to the demands of ordinary life upon it. The spread of supersensible knowledge ... is one of the tasks of the moment and the immediate future.
Rudolf Steiner: *A Road to Self-knowledge*

Are we in a post-Christian age?

It is becoming increasingly clear that Christendom, as part of western civilization in general, is facing a fatal downturn; a downward slide into a treacherous morass of shallow familiarity, slick sentimentality and dull dogma. If there is to be a resurgence the remedy must be the transformation of intellectualistic knowledge into spiritual knowledge. Faith alone cannot engender knowledge, and neither can belief, as these factors are hampered by lack of genuine forward development. We live in a scientific age when knowledge is sought, put to the test of proof, and either accepted or rejected. This procedure is tried and trusted, whereas beliefs which cannot always be supported by reason and supporting evidence therefore tend to foster mere opinion, and there is also danger of weakness by splitting into factions and sects.

For many people compliantly content with what information they are given rather than finding out for themselves, the Gospels of Matthew, Mark, Luke and John represent biographies outlining the life and teachings of a remarkable man called Jesus, how he went about doing good, giving practical advice for building up healthy communities, telling parables and performing remarkable healings and even miracles. Not unnaturally, he became very popular with the general public of his day, but not with the religious institutions, whose intrigues brought about his death by crucifixion. This is teaching at Sunday-school level, but most people remain at this elementary standing throughout their lives. The Gospel stories attract attention at both an emotional and a moral level, but the rapidly declining church attendance figures tell their own story—that of misgivings about what people are expected to believe and, to a certain extent, how to behave.

What Christianity needs is supportive evidence in the shape of valid knowledge, of a kind that is capable of transmuting its beliefs into understanding. Herein lies the danger of the expectation to believe whatever presents as learning through instruction from dubious sources of whatever kind. Persuasion involves trust, in matters as insecure as received religious doctrine, and necessarily involves possession of knowledge, which incorporates belief whilst progressing beyond it. A fresh kind of faith is needed that embraces newly available truths of a genuinely spiritual origin and nature; the present rigidified beliefs do not encompass them, and they are all too often oversimplified to the point of worthlessness, not to say garbled and misconstrued. Christianity as it is today is in danger of becoming de-spiritualized, worn out and self-discredited. It has lost its way in the present materialistic age simply because it has no answer to it, and this because as a creed it is intellectually frail and emotionally overweight. It has lost its role and its appeal, and must regain these by enriching what is essentially spiritual by discarding its materialistic baggage.

Much of the problem rests on the widespread inability to distinguish between Jesus of Nazareth and Jesus the Christ. Emphasis is being placed increasingly on Jesus the man rather than Jesus the Christ. Robert Reisenman, in his book *James, the Brother of Jesus,* emphasizes the lack of reliability that can be placed on the manner in which Gospel accounts are now widely construed. To take the texts as they seem rather than what they are is most unwise, for the problems with regard to translating them are greater than most people who rely on them in blind faith realize. The emphasis on reference to historical details is therefore quite misplaced, and this fact is being acknowledged by growing numbers of biblical scholars.

Inevitably, as time has gone on, and as techniques of analysis and examination, appraisal and deduction have become increasingly intellectual, misapprehensions have multiplied. It is all too easy for contemporary thinkers to construct rationalizations in order to satisfy their thirst to understand things in a purely intellectual way, but this is dangerous. It is of course in stark contrast to the language of mysticism, poetic and artistic imagery, metaphor and personification, which was the stock-in-trade of those early chroniclers, but these are now somewhat inappropriate. Christianity must learn to match the science of matter with a science of the spirit, and this has been proven to be possible; otherwise, there can be no resurgence from the present descent into dereliction. It is all too often forgotten that 'God is a Spirit'—and so are we all.

Other sources than the Scriptures?

One of Rudolf Steiner's many abilities was that of researching past, even long past, events occurring in the material world by 'reading the Akashic Records' or 'world memory'. In consequence, such investigations he undertook by this means were as accurate and sound as those made by research scientists into the material world. He was no woolly-minded mystic, but a scientist of the spirit who invited all who wished to put his findings to the test for corroboration. His researches into the Gospels and biblical Scriptures generally bear the stamp of authenticity: his findings, as amply substantiated in other chapters, are consistent and intersupportive. In short, they add up. The devoted work of biblical scholars who have meticulously analysed, by employing such methods as textual criticism and form criticism to examine similarities and differences among the so-called Synoptic Gospels of Matthew, Mark and Luke, counts for very little in reality. They do reveal, however, the fact that the Gospel of John, which is very different in character from the other three, is also more profound.

Steiner made so bold as to maintain that the events described in all four Gospels cannot be fully appreciated without the insights provided by the Akashic Records, and access to and understanding of these will come about of themselves in the course of evolution. The time will come, he declared, when people will be able, in the course of evolution, to dispense with the Bible altogether, becoming aware of its contents by means of natural clairvoyance—investigation into supersensory realms will be possible by direct spiritual perception.

A pervading theme throughout much spiritual-scientific knowledge and endeavour involves what Steiner called the Christ Event, by which he meant all effects and consequences of the mission on earth of the Christ as an exalted spiritual Being as Saviour and Redeemer of fallen mankind. However simple and straightforward acknowledgement and acceptance of this might be, it also marks a unique feature, namely, the direct involvement of heavenly spiritual beings with earthly humanity. As the Gospels infer time and time again, there are many mysteries also which involve the heavenly hosts, most of which remain 'hidden' to those who at present are not worthy of them. Contentious—and perhaps impudent—as the following observation might appear, it is nevertheless true, and remains subject to confirmation by scriptural evidence which will be offered in due course.

Steiner contended that his contribution in the shape of his book *The Fifth Gospel*—of which more anon—could justifiably be ranked alongside the four canonical Gospels, if for no other reason than that his methods of arriving at the contents of his findings were precisely those employed for the most part by the four Evangelists. He confirmed that they wrote their Gospels with the added benefit of genuine clairvoyance rather than ordinary sense-perception and other means, thus revealing their ability to avail themselves of the so-called Akashic Records or Cosmic Memory at will, as indeed he could and did. Thus he could justifiably claim to have employed the same means and methods as the four Evangelists; in effect, therefore, his 'Gospel' is as 'old' as theirs, in the sense that it was acquired in the same fashion and by the same means as they did. As was his unwavering policy, he placed no reliance on any kind of external evidence in the form of documents, archaeological artefacts and suchlike; although he often referred to these as appropriate, he took full responsibility for his own spiritual investigations.

His extraordinarily original and striking accomplishments in the domains of the Old Testament as well as the New Testament Scriptures were for the most part summarily dismissed as and when they appeared, and have been completely disregarded by orthodox theologians since, which attitude is not to their credit. Admittedly, his findings, based on his researches into the normally invisible, intangible realms, are so remarkably innovative that at first sight they often excite only ridicule and scorn, and are dismissed out of hand. He was, however, sufficiently confident in his methods and results as to challenge all comers to test his conclusions.

In any event, his work as philosopher, scientist, educationist, sociologist and universal man is becoming increasingly, if slowly, acknowledged. All he asked of his enquirers was open-mindedness and lack of prejudice. The reasons for this widespread reluctance is reflected in the public psyche as intolerance towards new ideas, and as Steiner's work was mainly concerned with issues of a spiritual nature, it induced certain antagonistic reactions ranging from scientific scepticism to religious bigotry. As ever, that which is not understood tends to be feared or denied, usually without reason, and this is often the case with spiritual science.

An important issue which is not afforded the concern it merits involves the widespread lack of discrimination with regard to Jesus the man and Jesus the Christ. The 'simple carpenter of Nazareth' is being increasingly acknowledged as the son of Mary and Joseph rather than the Christ Being as holy Son of God. To take the Gospel texts simply as they are would be most unwise, and the problems with regard to translating them are far greater than most people who rely on them in blind faith realize. The usual emphasis on reference to historical details is quite misplaced, a fact that is being acknowledged increasingly by biblical scholars. Unconventional as it may seem, the 'historical Jesus' may best be approached by way of the 'Cosmic Christ', an approach likely to be foreign to them, despite the many references to 'the Lord out of Heaven', 'heavenly hosts', and suchlike in both Testaments.

Christ Jesus was 'declared to be the Son of God with power, according to the spirit of holiness, by the resurrection from the dead' (Romans 1:4). This claim thus validates the notion that the Incarnation took place at the baptism in the River Jordan of Jesus of Nazareth by John the Baptist. This assertion represents a key reason for further authentication tracing back from the resurrection to the trial by Pilate, when he declared that his kingdom was 'not of this world' (John 18:36). Previously, at the actual baptism, John the Baptist 'bare record' that he whom he had baptized was indeed 'the Son of God'. This same expression was used by the angel who announced to Mary that her son shall be called Jesus, and 'the Son of the Highest' (Luke 1:32) and that the 'holy thing which shall be born of thee *shall be* called "the Son of God" ' (1:35). This declaration, be it noted, was made of the Luke Jesus, and it will be recalled that it is this Jesus boy who grew up as Jesus of Nazareth and was eventually baptized by John and declared 'the Son of God'.

In Matthew's Gospel the very first verse of the first chapter declares that the individual whose genealogy he was about to give was that of 'Jesus Christ', modified at 1:16 to 'Jesus who is called Christ'. As for sonship, the Matthew Jesus is proclaimed to be 'the son of David' and later taken to be 'King of the Jews' (Matthew 2:2). This Jesus boy did not survive, as we shall see, for he who is identifiable as Jesus of Nazareth was the Luke Jesus boy, whose genealogy is traced right back to God himself (Luke 3:38). It is posited that it was the Luke Jesus who became known as Jesus of Nazareth, and that this event occurred at the time of the Passover visit of the Luke parents to the temple in Jerusalem. The person later acknowledged as Jesus of Nazareth necessarily involved the natures and properties of *both* individuals—the two boys *in combination.* Corroborating inferences are there in the Gospel texts, and these, together with further supporting evidence, will be subjected to close scrutiny in due course.

The existence of two radically disparate Gospel accounts are there in the New Testament documents, and their very presence must be respected, irrespective of the fact that they cannot be reconciled, despite failed attempts to do so by certain tidy-minded scholars. The texts clearly demonstrate that there were indeed two Jesuses and not one, and to start with, two families: two Josephs, two Marys, and two Jesuses. All the efforts of some scholars to conflate them have proved fruitless; they have done their honest best according to their lights, and all the work they have put in to arrive at some kind of reconciliation of the Matthew and Luke accounts must be acknowledged, notwithstanding the fact that it amounts to the blind leading the blind. At the same time, they deserve to be reproached for failing to take seriously the earnest efforts of Rudolf Steiner to explain the differences between the two Gospel accounts. He was much abused and reviled when, in the early decades of the twentieth century, he made so bold as to set about explaining their disparities concerning these among many other discrepancies and enigmas that are to be found in biblical Scriptures.

Unbelief must be suspended

Here again it is necessary to apply the 'believe in order to understand' principle, for if esoteric truths and actualities are presented clearly and backed up with reason, evidence and example, they may simply not be believed on account of their sheer originality. Straightforward refusal even to consider such issues amounts to sheer prejudice, which would flatly deny that such a thing as esoteric knowledge exists. Steiner asserted that most esoteric knowledge has built-in defences against its becoming exoteric. In effect, it is a matter of those who have ears to hear hearing, and having eyes to see seeing. Those who can hear and see are able to make sense of whatever truths are presented, and therefore have the advantage over those capable of apprehending matters to only a limited extent. Some truths are therefore hidden to them and will remain so until the necessary ancillary knowledge is gained.

In the past there were very good reasons for the unprepared masses to remain ignorant of truths that are difficult to grasp. In Matthew (13:10–13) we read: 'And the disciples came, and said unto him [Jesus]: Why speakest thou in parables? He answered and said unto them, Because it is given to you to know the mysteries of the kingdom of heaven, but to them it is not given. For whosoever hath, to him shall be given, and he shall have more abundance: but whosoever hath not, from him shall be taken away even that he hath. Therefore I speak to them in parables: because they seeing see not; and hearing they hear not, neither do they understand.' The populace in those times were offered only what they could cope with; nowadays all kinds of dubious, so-called esoteric knowledge is being peddled, and much harm has been done; but the time has now come when people must be allowed to proceed according to their own devices and their own lights.

Paul, in an early letter to the Corinthians (I, 3:1–2), wrote: 'And I, brethren, could not speak unto you as unto spiritual, but as unto carnal, even as unto babes in Christ. I have fed you with milk, and not with meat; for hitherto ye were not able to bear it, neither yet now are ye able.' Humanity is constantly evolving, however, and in the course of time 'all things will be made new', and the signs are clear. In the so-called *Gospel of Thomas* (81:10–14) appear the words: 'Jesus said: Know what is hidden before your face, and what is hidden from you will be revealed to you: for there is nothing hidden which will not be manifest.' Similar statements are to be found in Matthew 10:26, Mark 4:22 and Luke 8:17.

A very real help in any approach to these enormously complex and intricate matters is, if at all possible, to learn to recognize whatever is *archetypal* in their content, for these disclose reliable concepts that are thoroughly dependable. It is good and advisable to seek out and acknowledge *general truths*, and learn to recognize various spiritual laws which are made manifest. These make their appearance in the many correlations, parallels and other connections within and between the elegant models and patterns which frequently emerge. General principles and their functions inherent in such laws as polarities and their equilibrium, metamorphosis and transmutation, recurrence and recapitulation, reversal and reciprocity may be at work, but then may not be recognized and so not be understood by those who are unaware of them.

Luke reveals himself in his Gospel as possessing clairvoyant powers, as indeed do the other three Evangelists. However, he deliberately makes this fact plain during his short introduction (Luke 1:1–4) to his Gospel for the benefit of a certain Theophilus (Lover of God), to whom he also addresses his account of those early goings-on in the shape of the Acts of the Holy Apostles. It is apparent that from time to time Luke discloses himself as a prudent, even canny writer, and some words and expressions he employs create problems for translators in their difficult task of interpretation. Two examples of such a predicament are to be found in his short prologue to his Gospel.

Firstly, the word *autoptai* (literally self-seers) is, reasonably enough given the circumstances, translated as 'eyewitnesses', that is to say, those who were present at such and such occasion and reported what they saw and experienced. But this statement should alert us at once, if the term 'eyewitness' is thus construed, as being rather strange, because the only Evangelist who could possibly claim this was John. The three 'Synoptists' drew much from oral tradition and were definitely not present to witness events for themselves. Steiner, however, asserted that it refers to the fact that Luke was an initiate and clairvoyant, perhaps more advanced than the other 'Synoptists', Matthew and Mark. He commented that each of the Evangelists apprehended the same past events clairvoyantly in different ways, likening the situation to four people viewing the same tree from four different sides. Just as one person is incapable of seeing all four quarters of the tree at the same time, so 'self-seers' may report rather differing perceptions, with each one possessing a validity and importance of its own. Moreover, as Steiner had the advantage of possessing such attributes himself, and recognizing the jargon involved, he was also able more fully to appreciate reports of such investigations.

Secondly, another word in the introduction that may be rendered otherwise than the usual is *anothen,* more commonly interpreted as 'from the very first' rather than the alternative rendering 'from the beginning' or the like. This translation seems to be stating the obvious, for only an incompetent or unenlightened reporter would start anywhere else. However, it also means 'from above', that is to say, the spiritual world, the heavenly realms. The literal rendering of 'having had a perfect understanding of all things from the very first' might just as properly be worded: 'having been acquainted from above how to trace out (or examine) all things accurately'.

About the texts

A bothersome element to some Bible readers is the undeniably artistic patterns discernible in the Gospels. The Old Testament Scriptures contain much in the way of metaphor and simile, and this kind of language persisted. A literary heritage which contains references to mountains skipping like rams, and little hills like lambs (Psalms 114; Isaiah 55:12) tells of hills breaking forth into song, and the trees clapping their hands, and so on. Poetic licence is warranted when appropriate to the circumstances, for artistic presentations can be every bit as informative as dry and objective factual details. Every book in the Bible has been taken apart by the various 'experts', chapter by chapter, line by line, word for word by etymologists, textual and form critics, historians, archaeologists and every other breed of analyst. However, a culture which could boast barely a scrap of either science or philosophy can hardly be expected to express itself in other ways than it did. The literary and other devices of expression in both Old and New Testaments share common ground, as the many proof-texts and other cross-references amply demonstrate. Strange as it may seem, the search for the 'historical Jesus', for example, must extend to realms other than the earthly.

It is a common misconception—probably because of the scriptural order in the New Testament—that the letters of

Paul were written later than the Gospels. Born about AD 10 in Tarsus, Paul (as Saul) was bilingual, in Hebrew and Greek, and was educated as a Pharisee. His famous Damascus experience happened at about AD 34, his letters to the various churches falling within the time-frame AD 50–65. The traditional belief contended that he was martyred by execution in Rome in AD 67 or thereabouts and thus before even the first words of Mark were written.

It must be said that everything that may be construed as 'history' concerning the Gospels should be approached with the utmost caution. All biblical scholars warn of this, for fundamentalism in these respects has no foundation. The Gospels were not written entirely on the basis of the authenticity of events, although many external 'facts' are correct. The external circumstances, places and dates in any of the Gospels should not be taken as hard fact, as 'gospel'. In respect of Jesus' birth neither the place and the date nor the political or social circumstances can be regarded as certainties. The disputes and doubtings such as mentioned at John 7:41–2 should serve as a warning to all who wish for everything to be neat and tidy. With all this in mind, it is worth repeating that Rudolf Steiner maintained that the events described in all four Gospels cannot be fully appreciated without the insights provided by the Akashic Records. Needless to say, most orthodox scholars do not accept such an assertion.

The Church Father Irenaeus, who was born in 130 or thereabouts, and succeeded the martyred Pothinus as Bishop of Lyons in 177, was able to authenticate certain aspects concerning the gospellers. In his younger days he had been a pupil of Polycarp (c. 70–155), a much loved and respected individual who was on close and friendly terms with John the

Evangelist whilst he was in Ephesus writing the Book of Revelation. He used to reminisce about his association with John, and relate his words. In his treatise *Against Heresies* Irenaeus (*c*. 130–200) reported:

Matthew issued a written Gospel among the Hebrews in their own dialect, while Peter and Paul were preaching at Rome and laying the foundations of the Church. After their departure, Mark, the disciple and interpreter of Peter, also handed down to us in writing what had been preached by Peter. Luke, the companion of Paul, recorded in a book the Gospel preached by him. Afterwards John, the disciple of the Lord who also leaned upon his breast, did himself publish a Gospel during his residence at Ephesus in Asia.

In general, the Synoptic Gospels are concerned mainly with the Jesus as Son of Man, whilst John's Gospel deals primarily with the Christ as Son of God. The Gospels were composed some 30 or 40 years after the crucifixion. Mark's Gospel is usually dated at *c*. AD 70, and the Gospels of Matthew and Luke at sometime during the following decade. John's Gospel is dated later, between then and his death at Ephesus in AD 100.

The Gospel of Matthew, not unexpectedly more so than the other Gospels, has long been regarded as a collection of Messianic and other scriptural proof-texts taken out of context and made to serve his purposes. Certain details do have historical validation, as borne out by Josephus and others. The census called by Quirinius (Cyrenius), the Roman governor in Syria, in 6 or 7 AD substantiates Luke's dating of the birth of the Jesus (2:1) who descended from Nathan. Matthew's Jesus, traceable back to Solomon, was born some time before the death of Herod in 4 BC. Without committing himself to a firm date, Rudolf Steiner contended that the timescale between the two births was a matter of months, and this is reasonable given the circumstances at the time.

Matthew's Gospel, originally written in Aramaic and intended for the Hebrews, not unnaturally shows opposition to the occupying Romans. His nativity account is sober and workmanlike; he emphasizes the male element, and creates an atmosphere of darkness and death. Joseph receives heaven-inspired messages in the form of dreams, and has Jesus born in a house, and his royal ancestry is emphasized by the references to the Magi, the 'Three Wise Men' who by tradition were also of aristocratic breeding. Matthew's Jesus descended from David via Solomon, the first King of Israel, and was important enough to incite King Herod to take steps to kill him, but his plans were foiled after warnings to Joseph in a dream, and he was able to escape to Egypt with his family, evidently before the notorious 'massacre of the innocents' took place.

It is widely accepted that Mark's Gospel, the shortest of the four canonical Gospels, was written for the unlikely benefit of the Romans, and represents something of an attack on conventional Judaism. He immediately introduces John the Baptist and his good news of the arrival of the Son of Man. He is not at all concerned with genealogical matters, nativity stories and other such details.

Matthew's Gospel is generally understood to be a Greek translation of the text originally written in Hebrew. Like Mark, he is concerned with earthly kingdoms rather than heavenly. His Gospel opens with details of the descent of Jesus Christ, but starts with Abraham and ends with a curious reminder of this full appellation. It does not tally with

Luke's genealogy, which discrepancies will be discussed in Chapter 4.

Luke's Gospel is considerably longer than the others, and is not so much concerned with earthly kingdoms as with the Kingdom of Heaven. In it he is very much concerned with Mary, who is visited by angelic beings in broad daylight. The annunciation of her son's conception was made by an angel, and there is much mention of priests and temples, and holy things in general. Luke's Jesus was descended from David via Nathan, himself a priest, and his birth was attended by heavenly choirs, and the fact that David had once been a shepherd boy is echoed by the presence of shepherds at the manger in Bethlehem.

John's Gospel is quite different from the other three, and lays great stress on the fact that a new impulse had entered the world, signalling a long-awaited New Age. John's Gospel addresses the spiritual in mankind rather than the worldly. His extraordinary prologue concerning the Word as the pre-existent Christ is swiftly followed by the baptism of the Christ, an event which corresponds to some kind of divine birth process. There is no nativity story in this Gospel, which is altogether more sophisticated than those of the Synoptic Gospels, and is demanding of appreciation at a higher level. There is no mention of parables, for instance, and the 'miracle' of the raising of Lazarus is obviously meant to be construed in mystical rather than profane terms. Of the Evangelists, it was John, 'the disciple whom Jesus loved', who was personally acquainted with Christ Jesus, which implies that his Gospel might well be regarded as the most author-itative. The very last verse but one suggests this, but even so, as with the three Synoptic Gospels, caution is necessary. Without doubt, many of the events mentioned did take place, and are subject to verification in the usual ways, but at the same time they cannot be said to have depended to any appreciable extent on external or 'secondary' evidence to back up the narratives.

The Fifth Gospel

It may seem presumptuous for someone to make public a book with this title based on lecture courses, but this is what Rudolf Steiner saw fit to do—and for sound and valid reasons. They were given to members only of the newly established Anthroposophical Society in the autumn of 1913, firstly in Oslo and soon after in various cities in Germany. He maintained that he gave these lectures 'out of an inner obligation', and not for any other reason, considering that the matters dealt within them to be publicized as a kind of historical necessity. He admitted feeling a certain reluctance, and fully anticipated the hostility that their divulgence would arouse, but nevertheless he declared that it was 'essential that knowledge of such facts should now flow into Earth evolution'.

It would be an impossible task to attempt any substantial treatment of Steiner's remarkable book, for its range is very broad; moreover, it presupposes that his readers possess a fair knowledge of the basic premises and ideas of anthroposophical spiritual science. For the most part it deals with the so-called 'lost 18 years' of the life of Jesus of Nazareth from the well-known temple episode described in Luke's Gospel at 2:41–52 and his baptism in the River Jordan. Nothing of these years is reported by any of the four Gospel writers, and this gap in the 'history' of Jesus has intrigued many generations of biblical scholars, and no account has emerged from any reliable quarter either. Needless to say, perhaps, Steiner's version, the source of which was the Akashic Records, has not found a shred of acceptance by orthodox theologians. This is somewhat unfortunate on their part, as he mentions many aspects of interest, ranging from fascinating details of Jesus' conversations with his mother to intriguing descriptions of the Essene community—and this long before the so-called Dead Sea Scrolls were discovered. *The Fifth Gospel*, however, read in conjunction with the canonical Gospels themselves in the light of Steiner's whole treatment of the 'two Jesuses' problem, approached open-mindedly, makes complete sense. Moreover, it could well be for many people the very catalyst that could reinvigorate a dying Christianity. Steiner's work, which is at once factually sound and intellectually satisfying, rests on knowledge rather than belief.

Plainly, the main weakness of religious faiths of every persuasion is undoubtedly their weakness of structure. In this Christianity stands out from all others, not because of its teachings, which after all differ very little in essence from other religions, but because it acknowledges the direct involvement of an exalted spiritual Being, namely, the Christ Being. This Being has been identified as a member of the *Exousiai*, or Spirits or Form, referred to in the New Testament as Authorities. The early Christians knew this, and they understood that what might with justification be called the New Mysteries were as much to do with the cosmos as with the earth. The manner in which the Christian Church developed, however, gradually brought about the loss of its cosmic associations. In short, nowadays its emphasis is on Jesus the earthly man rather than Christ the exalted spiritual Being, whereas many of the other religions lack sufficient knowledge and do not claim heavenly connections except in vague and confused ways.

The appellation 'God' bears different meanings for the various religions throughout the world, and indeed for every individual person. He is therefore accorded qualities that suit people's general world-outlook. The various religious interests and concerns involve God as their adherents understand him—more correctly 'it', in the sense of the Great Universal or All-embracing Spirit—and organized Christianity has followed this trend. Admittedly, the God of the Bible is reckoned to exist in the heavenly worlds, but when pressed for details Christians tend to be nonplussed. This suggests that their religious concepts arise rather from their imaginations and not in veritable reality. With no agreement about this matter, small wonder that schisms appeared—opposing opinions rather than a certainty of facts. Reference was made earlier to the necessity for some kind of structure even in matters of faith and belief, and this in turn emphasizes the need for *knowledge* as support for considerations such as these, and spiritual science seeks to provide it.

Christ as one of the Elohim

The connections between the first five verses of the first chapter of John's Gospel and the first five of Genesis are clear; even the first three words 'In the beginning' are the same. In Genesis we are left in no doubt that it was 'God', or more correctly 'the Gods', as this is the literal translation of the Hebrew word *Elohim* (a collective noun which takes the singular) who created the heavens and the earth. The latter was nevertheless quite without *form* and void, and there was nothing but darkness all around. God had only to *say* 'Let there be light' for it to come about. In John's Gospel all this is taken for granted and at the same time God's spoken commands are elaborated upon by the statement that the 'Word' was of divine nature, and moreover *creative*. The Greek word *logos* has many applications, but its root conveys the general idea of the word by which an inward thought is expressed outwardly, and thus by inference creatively.

These obvious parallels between the first few verses of Genesis and those of John's Gospel tell their own story, but there are deeper meanings also. John's actual words are enigmatic, and for this reason alone we should be on our guard: if the Word was 'with' God, as in the Authorized Version, the New English Bible and the Jerusalem Bible among others, what kind of sense does it make to state that the Word actually was God? The literal Greek runs: '. . . *kai theos en ho logos*', word for word 'and God was the Word'. However, the Authorized Version has it 'and the Word was God'—the other way round. The New English Bible, sensing the trickiness of the problem, has 'and what God was, the Word was'. This is still not good enough, however. Now the indefinite article does not exist in New Testament Greek; nevertheless, it is inserted by translators if they consider it appropriate to do so. If we construe the situation somewhat differently, and see fit to place an indefinite article between 'and' and 'God', so that the passage reads 'and (*a*) God was the Word' the predicament is resolved without resorting to stratagem. It makes more sense to state 'a God was the Word'—for this accords with the Greek text—rather than simply 'God was the word'. John had already made clear that the entity in question was already with God, and we might therefore be entitled to accuse the Logos as being part of God rather than declaring that an entity was *being something as well as being with* that something. It could seem that either John was being deliberately tautologous or translators are unwilling to acknowledge the lack of the indefinite article in order to make everything plain. More apparently needless repetition immediately follows. The Authorized Version has: 'All things were made by him, and without him there was not any thing made that was made.' The New English Bible comes up with the somewhat inelegant 'and through him all things came to be; no single thing was created without him'. A more literal translation, however awkward, would be: 'All things came into being through him, and without him came into being not even one (single) (thing) which has come into being.'

The Hebrew word for God is *Elohim,* well known as an example of a plural noun governing the singular number in terms of grammar. Thus when in Genesis 1:26 God says, 'Let us make man(kind) in our own image, after our likeness, and let them have dominion...' the plurality of the Elohim is revealed, who severally bestow their gifts. At Genesis 2:4, the appellation 'Lord God' is introduced, and there has been much discussion among theologians as to the two apparent 'strands' that emerge, the 'Elohist' and the 'Yahwist', and these have been followed with application and zeal, but to small overall profit. Rather, the situation seems to be echoed in St John's Gospel, where the Word is 'with God' as well as being (a) 'god' in his own right. The similarities are certainly too significant to be ignored: 'I and the Father are one' (John 10:30). In John 8:58 Christ himself, by saying 'Verily, verily, I say unto you, Before Abraham was, I am,' sees fit to affirm emphatically that he was pre-existent, as the Elohim were (or was). Paul (Philippians 2:5–6) also makes this clear by observing that the Christ is 'equal with God'; indeed, according to Steiner, he was one of the Elohim.

The Elohim are members of the third rank of the Second Hierarchy, the *Exousiai*, commonly translated as Authorities or Powers. Rudolf Steiner adopted the name Spirits of Form, which is descriptive of their function in relation to their role in earthly matters. In Genesis the world has been created, but is 'without form and void' (Genesis 1:2). What could be more fitting than for the Spirits of Form to set about formulating the necessary archetypes, prototypes and other such foundational factors as appropriate and necessary to allow for metamorphosis and advancement in the shape of principles of evolution? Taken together, the first verses of Genesis and the opening sentences of John's Gospel seem to fit very nicely. What emerges from such considerations is the contention that the Word of the New Testament is none other than the Yahweh of the Old Testament. In other words, the Christ Being, as a 'leading' member of the Exousiai, is also the 'Lord God' of the Elohim, which were seven in number. The Greek word generally translated as 'Lord' is *kyrios*, a title used in Mystery Centres to refer to the Sungod, to be adopted in subsequent times to refer to Christ Jesus, or even to Jesus plain and simple.

The Son and the sun

The sun, as we all know is the source, direct and indirect, of all that manifests as light in our planetary world; that it should figure large in all aspects of the life and culture of our forefathers is readily understandable. The initiated priests within the ancient Mysteries knew that the sublime Sun-god of whom they spoke was the same Being who in due time would be acknowledged as the Christ, 'the Light of the

World'. This, however, could only be after he had 'descended' and incarnated in the physical body of Jesus of Nazareth at his baptism by John in the River Jordan—the Christ as Sun-god, having now appeared on earth, could no longer be present in the sun. It was his mission to unite himself with the earth and its human inhabitants: 'Lo, I am with you always, even unto the end of the age' (Matthew 28:20). In his declaration that his kingdom was not of this world (John 18:36) Christ Jesus made it plain that he had come from other, cosmic or heavenly realms.

The oracle establishments were preserved from prehistoric times as far back as the Atlantean epoch. The guardian of the Sun oracle was Zarathustra or Zoroaster, who lived in much earlier times than the individual of the same name who founded the Magian system of religion in Persia in the sixth century BC. Zarathustra lived during the period during which the ancient Persian civilization was thriving, i.e. 5000–3000 BC. The historical Zarathustra divulged to his people that the exalted Sun or Light Spirit, otherwise known as Ahura Mazda or Ormuzd, would later descend to earth and appear in human form as the Christ.

The teachings emanating from the Mystery Schools, as well as the long-held common tradition, maintained that the sun and the Light that radiated from it was supremely important. In fact, it was worshipped, revered and esteemed, but not only as a ball of fire in the heavens that made life itself possible on earth, but also the dwelling of an exalted Sun Being. The neophytes in the Mysteries were told that spiritual as well as ordinary light streamed from the sun, and that this stream, vitalized by the Sun Being himself, bore them beyond death into the spiritual worlds, and accompanied them until, eventually, they would return to the earth. They felt, and were conscious that, it was the Spirit of the Sun that gave them immortality.

In the lower orders of the Mysteries, the rites of which involved the general populace, the ritual was performed whereby an image of the Sun-god was laid into a grave and after three days it would be taken out again. This ceremony was symbolical in that the Sun-god is restored to life, and he was the Being who awakens every individual to life after death has occurred. The act of interment of the human image betokened descent into the earthly realms, from which eventually he rose again into fresh life.

The first chapter of John's Gospel (1:9) states: (The Word) 'was the true Light, which lighteth every man that cometh into the world.' The significance of light and the Sun-god in teachings are discussed in Chapter 3.

Steiner contended that John, who spent a considerable time at Ephesus, where he wrote the Book of Revelation, was well acquainted with Mystery teachings. It must not be forgotten that John was the disciple of Christ Jesus who 'leaned on his breast', and whom he 'loved'. This kind of language usage was especially meaningful to those in the higher orders of the Mysteries, marking John out as a high initiate. At 8:12 we read: 'Then spake Jesus ... I am the light of the world: he that followeth me shall not walk in darkness, but shall have the light of life'—that is to say, life after death.

In contrast to the Pharisees, and by inference the common people, Christ Jesus said: 'Though I bare record of myself, my record is true: for I know whence I came, and whither I go' (8:14). John, in these verses, employs the powerful symbols of light and darkness remarkably succinctly and to great effect. In his well-known prologue to his Gospel he is clearly seen to be speaking out of the tradition of Light and Darkness as archetypal entities dating from the times of Zarathustra during the ancient Persian Epoch. During that time the sun, in its retrogressive path around the earth, was transiting the zodiacal sign of Gemini or the Twins. Then was the time of duality, as its sign clearly shows: the upper hemispherical component represents the sky above, as the lower signifies the earth beneath. Separating these two hemispheres are two pillars; the symbols and their message could not be clearer, for as well as joining the hemispheres they are also holding them apart. The bright sky above and the dark earth below were personified by Ormuzd (Ahura Mazda), the great Sun-god and giver of light and life, who was constantly opposed by Ahriman, the god of darkness and death.

In the opening lines of his first epistle (verse 5) John affirmed that his declaration that 'God is light ... in which there is no darkness at all' came directly from Christ Jesus, and all allusions to Light and Darkness as exhibiting archetypal qualities were in total agreement with the Mystery teachings for the previous seven or eight centuries. In John 8:12 we read: 'Then spake Jesus again unto them, saying, I am the light of the world; he that followeth me shall not walk in darkness, but shall have the light of life,' thereby echoing the prologue to his Gospel (1:4): 'In him was life, and the life was the light of mankind.' Matthew, at 5:14–16 paralleled this in his report on the Sermon on the Mount when Jesus said to his disciples, 'Ye are the light of the world,' going on to say that even a candle is important in this respect. Paul and Barnabas managed to upset the Jews—whilst pleasing the Gentiles—with their hints which clearly smack of Mystery wisdom. The Evangelists Luke at Acts 13.47 and John at 8:12 both report the strong association of light with life from the lips of Jesus himself, as quoted above.

The many references to light in John's Gospel are reminders of the principle of light as a major concern of the Mystery Schools from the time of Zarathustra right through to that of the Evangelist's own times. At 23:24–36 John mentions 'sons of Light' and Paul says in I Thessalonians 5:5: 'Ye are all children of light, and the children of the day; we are not of the night, or of darkness.' There is Jesus himself, whose great concern with light attracted the unwelcome attention of the Jews, in that he was obliged to hide from them (John 12:35, 36). Paul and Barnabas had the temerity, also after upsetting the Jews by claiming that the Lord himself had appointed them 'to be a light of the Gentiles', were obliged to make a rapid exit (Acts 13:47–50). Paul, however, insisted on employing the typical language of the Mysteries, as in I Thessalonians 5:5: 'Ye are all children of light, and the children of the day; we are not of the night, nor of darkness.' He was steeped in such ideas, and in his letter to the Ephesians where he exhorts them to 'walk as children of light' (5:8) this again is typical Mysteries jargon.

The darkness of this and the coming age, which now has access to the 'light' of spiritual science, has lasted for a millennium and a half. John the Evangelist must have known that the Christ Impulse would not become fully active until the times of spiritual darkness, that is to say, the historical Dark Ages of the early centuries of the last millennium, which was followed by the ever-accelerating escalation of materialism, from the Age of Reason to the widespread acceptance of logical-positivism in modern times. The Light has been— and indeed still is—shining in the Darkness, but the time may now have come when the dawn of a new spirituality will penetrate our own murky times.

The 'Second Coming' enigma

To Rudolf Steiner the concept of a 'Second Coming' of the Christ was closely bound up with the Krishnamurti phenomenon. The notion that this exalted spiritual Being was foreordained to return to the earth and its inhabitants *in the flesh* he vigorously denounced, and it was mainly for this reason that he delivered the series of lectures on the Gospels. He declared emphatically that the mission of Christ as the Messiah, and all that this entailed, was a unique Event that could not and would not be repeated. He did not deny that a Second Coming would occur, but asserted that it would manifest in a manner very similar to that experienced by the apostle Paul on the road to Damascus. In short, when the 'risen Christ' ascended into the 'clouds', this refers to his 'ascent' into the etheric realms, which 'upwardly' adjoin our earthly realm. Henceforth it was there that he could be found, his mission on the earth having been completed. In fact, in a very real sense he had united himself with the earth and indeed its destiny. Hitherto he could be sought and found only on the sun, as had long been known in the Mystery Centres, hence the constant references to the sun and its light over the preceding ages. Now, however, he was to make himself 'accessible' to all humanity: 'And lo, I am with you all the days until the completion of the age' (Matthew 18:20). Naturally, the question arises: how, by what means may the Christ Being be accessed?

In his lecture cycle published as *The Christ Mystery in Relation to the Secret of Pentecost*, Steiner argues that until the fourth century people were still aware that Christ who was the Being of the Sun and Christ who lived in Jesus of Nazareth were one and the same Being. After that time there came to be more and more attention paid to Jesus Christ mainly as a historical figure. The whole Christ Event was a spiritual as well as an outer occurrence, and moreover one that was unique, that is to say, a one-off event never to be repeated. Now, two thousand years later, it is only when individuals are ready to seek the spiritual world that they will find the Christ as an ever-present reality, and this seeking is right and necessary for humankind now and in future times. When people reject the existence of spiritual worlds they are in danger of losing the Christ. If they earnestly strive towards these worlds, it will eventually be revealed to them that Christ is not only the Being who lived two thousand years ago in Palestine, but is also the living Christ who dwells on—or even, it may be said, actually in—the earth and amid us now.

As an initiate into the Hebrew Mysteries, Paul—or rather Saul—could not bring himself to acknowledge that the Messiah had indeed arrived on earth in the physical body of Jesus of Nazareth. On the occasion of his 'Damascus experience', however, he came to realize that the Christ as Messiah would henceforth be perceived in the sphere of the earth or, more precisely, the etheric realms which pervades and surrounds it. Rudolf Steiner, as a diligent researcher into the Christian Mysteries, posited three sources of knowledge concerning them. First of all is that contained within the Gospels and the traditions associated with them. Second, there are the sources accessed by means of genuine clairvoyance and spiritual insights. Of the third, he had this to say in his book *From Jesus to Christ:*

And now from the twentieth century onwards a third source begins. It arises because an ever-increasing number of people will experience an extension, an enhancement of the intellectual powers which is *not* brought about through meditation, concentration and other exercises. As we have often said, more and more individuals will be able to renew for themselves the event of Paul on the road to Damascus. Thereby a period will begin of which we can say that it will provide a direct means of perceiving the significance and the Being of Christ Jesus.

(Note: Detailed comment on this statement is not practicable in present circumstances. Such an experience that Steiner describes here would in any case be a highly personal one, which event would take place in a shape or form appropriate to each individual person's stage of spiritual development. It is perfectly possible for someone to undergo spiritual experiences of various kinds, mostly of a low order, almost without recognizing them for what they are. In the present atmosphere of scepticism where spiritual matters are concerned, and blunted sensibilities due to 'sensory overload' and the numberless distractions that are part of our modern lifestyles, many people may well fail to understand what was actually occurring.)

In the same course of lectures Steiner went on to contend that, in addition, another important event will occur at the same time, namely, that the Christ becomes the Lord of Karma for human evolution. In support of this, he quoted Acts 10:42 '... to testify that it is he which was ordained of God *to be* the Judge of the quick and the dead', and this same statement appears in Acts 17:31, John 5:22, 27; Romans 14:9–10; II Corinthians 5:10, II Timothy 4:1, and I Peter 4:5. There can be no doubt concerning this as it is inferred in many other statements.

He also pointed out as highly significant the sacking of

Jerusalem by the Romans in AD 70. The magnificent Solomon's Temple, representing as it did the whole Old Testament world-conception, its conformity to law, its message, purpose and ethos, was destroyed soon after the Christ Event. It had now served its purpose, and henceforth everything would be different. Christ had fulfilled his mission, for 'old things have passed away; behold, all things are become new' (II Corinthians 5:17; Revelation 21:5). Thus came about the prophecy of Isaiah 43:18–19: 'Remember ye not the former things, neither consider the things of old. Behold, I will do a new thing; now it shall spring forth; shall ye not know it?' This is reiterated by him at 65:17: 'For, behold, I create new heavens and a new earth: and the former shall not be remembered, nor come into mind.' In II Peter 3:13 we read: 'Nevertheless we, according to his promise, look for new heavens and a new earth, wherein dwelleth righteousness.' Thus the evolution of both mankind and the earth itself was influenced by this whole Christ Mystery, with repercussions throughout both seen and unseen worlds.

Was Jesus of Nazareth a member of the Essenes?

It must seem strange to many Christians that there was a very long gap indeed between the birth of the Messiah and his dramatic appearance on the world stage at the age of 30 or so, except for the brief mention of the temple incident at twelve years of age. It is barely credible that Jesus of Nazareth had failed to be recognized during this time, if indeed he had been Jesus Christ from birth, as is generally taught and understood, and being acknowledged as *Jesus the Christ* at his baptism, as 'adopted' at this time. If so, why did it take so long for him to be recognized as such? It is significant that he is recorded in all four Gospels as being recognized as the Messiah very soon after the baptism in the Jordan, and in no instance before that event (see Matthew 16:16; Mark 8:29; Luke 4:41; John 1:41).

Rudolf Steiner, in his *Fifth Gospel,* states that Jesus of Nazareth spent several years, including those leading up to his baptism, in the community of the Essenes, a Jewish monastic sect whose whole lifestyle was concentrated on aspects of spiritual development under a strict regime designed to this end. Had he been *born* the Son of God, the Sun of Righteousness, the Saviour and all the other things he was claimed to be, why did it take so long for all these facts to come to light? At the age of twelve he made a tremendous impression on the doctors of the law in the temple; why, then, do we not hear more of the 'lost years' in the career of this lad who stated quite openly that he expected his parents—and presumably the priests and scribes who must have been around—to know that he was 'about his Father's business' (Luke 2:49). The notion that his disappearance without trace for 18 years or so was presumably in order to prepare for his mission does not seem to be a matter of much interest to many Christians other than scholars.

The Essenes were a closed Palestinian sect with an esti-mated membership of about 4000 at the time of Christ. Their community required its members to lead a life that developed a higher life within the soul and so brought about a new birth. The aspirant was subjected to a severe test in order to ascertain whether he was mature enough to prepare himself for a higher life. If admitted, he was made to take a solemn oath that he would not betray to strangers the secrets of the community, and was required to undergo a period of pro-bation. Its purpose was the mastering of his lower nature, so that the spirit slumbering within him might be aroused and developed stage by stage thereafter.

Essenes were insistent that the 'Last Days' were nigh, that the old order had run its course, and that a completely New Age was about to begin. They were active devotees of the system of 'ascents' or grades on the ladder to perfection, and were skilled in astrology and astronomy, and were said to be able to forecast the deathday of members from study of their horoscope. It also seems that they were familiar with the actualities of reincarnation, for complete success at 'ascending' to perfection usually takes many lifetimes. Theirs was not blind belief in certain truths and dogmas, but faith in their own competence to attain the ability to experience the spiritual worlds for themselves.

The communities of Essenes and Therapeutae form a natural transition from the Mysteries to Christianity, which wished to extend to humanity at large what had been the affair of a sect. Thus what had been striven for in the narrower circle of the Mysteries had become the concern of a wider community. Robert Reisenman, in his book *James, the Brother of Jesus,* points out that the term 'Sons of Light' was one self-designation for the members of the Essene community at Qumran. This fact demonstrates that the knowledge of these doctrines and their identification with the 'Christ' comes before the Gospels in their present form. Furthermore, the notion of what he called the 'Primal Adam' ideology and the 'standing vocabulary' are mentioned in the Dead Sea Scrolls. This bears out Steiner's assertions, made long before the Scrolls were found, that the Essenes constituted a bridge from the Mysteries to Christianity.

The so-called Dead Sea Scrolls discovered at Qumran are believed to refer to this community who lived in a fortress-like building from the time of Alexander Jannaeus (103–76 BC) until about the time of the destruction of Jerusalem by the Romans in AD 70. They had a reputation for asceticism, and in any case were highly disciplined, holding their founder, the 'Teacher of Righteousness', in very high regard. Initiation, which included baptism, was practised. In anticipation of the 'Last Supper' to come, and echoing the meal provided for Abraham by Melchizedek, they shared in community meals of bread and wine. They expected two Messiahs, one kingly and the other priestly, and this fits in very neatly with the facts of the nativities as described by Matthew and Luke respectively, and which have been discussed in detail earlier.

Flavius Josephus, the prolific Jewish historian (AD 37–c. 100 +), should, one feels, have lived a generation earlier, for his account of the life of Jesus Christ is woefully brief. Jesus was a 'wise man, if it be lawful to call him a man, for he was a doer of wonderful works (. . .) He was (the) Christ (. . .) who was condemned to the cross by Pilate (but) appeared to (those that loved him) alive again the third day . . .' (*Antiquities of the Jews*, XVIII, iii, 3). Josephus also reports (XV, x, 5) that Herod held the Essenes in high regard, as indeed he himself did, probably 'because many of these Essenes have, by their excellent virtue, been thought worthy of [this] knowledge of divine revelation.' In view of even these scanty details, many a scholar has sighed wistfully, deploring the fact that Josephus was not around to report on the nativities and other details.

They regarded the Teacher of Righteousness as the inspired expositor of the divine Mysteries, who promulgated the conviction that the world is divided between the Sons of Light and the Children of Darkness, as did Zarathustra and his successors. The Essenes upheld what they taught, and adopted this Persian doctrine, which was that there is constant opposition between these powers. It is widely accepted that The Manual of Discipline is of Essene origin, and the following prophetic passage clearly refers to themselves: 'They shall be judged by the first judgments by which men of the community began to be disciplined, until there shall come a prophet (in the person of John the Baptist) and the Messiahs of Aaron (priestly) and Israel (kingly).' Similar passages are to be found in the Damascus Document, thus consolidating the fact that there were indeed two Jesus boys but only one Jesus of Nazareth.

3
MYSTERY CENTRES AND CHRISTIANITY

In spiritual science we are seeking the thoughts of the gods wherewith they have guided the course of evolution, and this creates in us a deep morality. Nowadays, knowledge of spiritual science not only brings us wisdom consciously rather than instinctively, as was formerly the case, but we receive a moral stimulus as well.

Rudolf Steiner

Worlds known and unknown

Our ancestors knew very well that they were inhabitants of two worlds—the heavenly and the earthly. Mythologies of every race, nation or people trace their origins to the heavenly worlds, the unseen worlds, the spiritual worlds. It is often difficult for us, surrounded as we are by a world that is solid and material, to imagine what our prehistoric forefathers experienced in their daily lives, and how they viewed nature and the universe. As they were aware of both worlds, they treated them as equally real. They gradually advanced to being guided, firstly by the gods themselves, and later by the heroes, the demigods who were able to commune with them.

Humanity, in those early millennia, very much depended on the leadership and guidance of such beings, whose work was gradually taken over by advanced individuals who adopted the role of priest-kings. They maintained their status by exercising their superior wisdom and knowledge in their role as leaders; but as their ability to commune directly with the 'higher' spiritual entities eventually faded, they came more and more to rely on custom and tradition. Ultimately, as secular affairs grew ever more important, only the factor of power remained, as echoed in the notion of 'the divine right of kings'. Thus the familiar duo of 'priestly' and the 'kingly' factors asserted themselves to an increasing extent, and with it misuse of pastoral authority by the first group and the corrupting attributes of sheer power wielded by the second.

However, the original purity of the spirituality and ethical integrity of those hierophants and their initiate associates was carefully preserved in the various Mystery Schools or Mystery Centres, which guarded in jealous fashion the secrets of the 'higher' unseen worlds. The wisdom that they inherited and attained to was jealously concealed from the people they led. This uniquely human attribute is absolutely imperative for training in spiritual advancement of any kind; there are no exceptions to this requirement.

As Rudolf Steiner asserted from his researches into the Akashic Records or 'World Memory', the consciousness of our forebears was dreamlike, lacking the sharpness and clarity that we ourselves experience in modern times. Indeed, it was the case that what we now know as death was not experienced as such by those early peoples as a total extinction of consciousness at a certain point in time, but rather as a change in general awareness. Their experience of the supersensory or spiritual worlds was little different in quality from that whilst sojourning in the world of the senses. When what might be called the 'illusion' of death occurred, that is, when they left their physical body when adverse circumstances obliged them to do so, their apprehension of the spiritual world widened to include the spiritual 'infrastructure' and workings of the entire universe—and this, of course, still obtains.

Steiner often described how it is that the sun and the planets, visible to us as material objects, are inhabited by various orders of spiritual beings. Needless to say, perhaps, it is the sun itself that is the most important. He asserted that it was the abode of the pre-existent Logos or Word, Christ himself, and that Christ was a member of the Second Hierarchy, that of the *Exousiai*, the biblical term for whom is Powers or Authorities (see Ephesians 3:10; 6:12). Steiner gave then the more descriptive name of Spirits of Form. Of the Christ Being, as the Word, it is written that 'through him all things came into being, and without him came into being not even one (thing) which has come into being' (John 1:1). This verse is preceded by the enigmatic 'In the beginning was the Word, and the Word was with God, and (a) God was the Word.' However this sentence is construed, there is no doubt about the credentials of the Christ as 'God of the Sun', upon which the very world itself depends for its ongoing existence.

True to the ancient truism 'As above, so below' and also 'As within, so without', we actually are cosmic beings as well as earthly beings. Steiner described in his lecture cycle *Mystery Centres* how things were in prehistoric times:

Only think for a moment how man lived ... still one with the cosmos, in unity with the cosmos. Today when man thinks, he has to think in isolation with his head. Within are his thoughts and his words come forth. The universe is outside. Words can only indicate the universe; thoughts can only reflect the universe. When man was still one with the cosmos this was not the case, for then he experienced the universe as if in himself. The Word was at the same time his environment. Man heard, and what he heard was the Word.

He often rendered his disclosures in artistic form, and for sound reasons. The issues under discussion serve as examples of this approach as employed by Steiner. Human nature actually does mirror the universe. Such notions are often difficult to express in readily comprehensible, finite terms without detailed prior acquaintance with them by readers. His endeavour was to arouse their own powers of appreciation of matters spiritual, and to indicate certain paths of further contemplation to this end. Their expression in poetic style is often preferable to prose in the interests of conciseness as well as to stimulate mental activity.

These short meditational verses are taken from Steiner's *Verses and Meditations:*

My Head bears the being of the resting Stars.
My Breast harbours the life of the wandering Stars.
My Body lives and moves amid the Elements.
This am I.

In the boundless Without
Find thyself, O Man!
In the innermost Within
Feel the boundless Worlds!
So will it be revealed:
Nowhere the Riddle of the World is solved
Save in the being of Man.

A diversity of gods

It is significant that Jesus Christ appeared on the earth at the very time when the Graeco-Roman civilization was at the peak of its development. The grand sweep of history from East to West, starting in India at about 8000 BC with the main thrust of development and culture taking place successively in Persia, Egypt and Babylonia, and thence to Greece and Rome, found the eastern Mediterranean basin a stable environment for the new religion of Christianity to establish itself. Rudolf Steiner maintained that this period, when the gods actually 'appeared' in human form, did not arrive as if by chance, but was purposely established by the Spiritual Hierarchies to familiarize humanity with the notion that one of their number would in very fact appear on the earth in human form. The evidence for this lies in the meticulous care with which this very special human body was prepared, that is to say, by the ancestors of the two Jesus children as set out in Matthew and Luke, about which Steiner had much to say in his lecture courses on the Gospels.

Both boys were born during the time of Augustus (63 BC–AD 14), the first of the Roman emperors, and with the *Pax Romana* came the spread of ideas and the development of commerce and trade. The Mediterranean shores were politically and culturally secure. The dominant languages were Latin in the western areas and *koine* Greek, the vernacular of the traders and also of the New Testament. At such a time, when interference of the gods in the affairs of human beings was considered normal and proper, there was no shortage of religions and sects professing diverse beliefs and claiming special powers and privileges for their followers.

The bestowing of divine status on outstanding leaders was common in those times, and both Alexander the Great and Augustus Caesar were accorded it almost as a matter of course. Local religious cults decayed or were amalgamated into others of like nature under the pressures of centralization of power and authority, and the well-known resistance by the Jews to the might and influence of Rome is an outstanding exception to this overwhelming trend. Wisely, the Roman authorities resisted the temptation to impose the imperial will too firmly on this strange people, whose religion remained stubbornly monotheistic in a world that was riddled with polytheistic religions of various kinds.

Prominent at these times, too, were the Mystery religions and cults, with their centres of learning and initiation into secret teachings. By definition, little is known about these Mystery Schools, for their members were sworn to secrecy on pain of death. Indeed, there is little doubt that some of them fostered standards of spiritual development of a very lofty nature, which in turn gave rise to ethical and behavioural standards of an equally high standard. This is not to say that there were not many sects and cults that were characterized by crude rites and practices, some of which were bizarre and certainly unacceptable by modern standards. The writer of The Book of Wisdom, commonly acknowledged to have been a Jew in the last century BC who was well acquainted with Greek culture, makes reference to typical decadent activities, such as 'child-murdering initiates, secret Mysteries, their orgies with outlandish ceremonies'. It is significant that he taught 'temperance, prudence, justice and fortitude', which reveals his acquaintance with certain ideas of Plato.

These Mystery Centres arose, for the most part, in the eastern regions of the Mediterranean rim. This is perhaps significant because civilization, in its progress westwards, had taken with it memories of the times when insights into the spiritual worlds were more reputable, as for example, in the case of the Hebrews, with their sophisticated system of devotion to one supreme god in the shape of Yahweh, and the ranks of spiritual beings that were subject to him. Persia, Syria and Egypt, as well as the Asia Minor peninsula with its strong Greek influences provided ideal locations for the Mystery Schools.

Many of their teachings centred on a saviour-god who had died and risen again; and the names of the various gods involved, and their deeds, differed rather more in detail than in substance. All these are the stuff of mythology, but they were not, as is often popularly supposed nowadays, mere fantasies, products of human imagination and fancy. Rather were they echoes of even earlier times when perception of the supersensible worlds was consciously sought and developed by our ancestors, and they obtained true insights into the outer world of nature and their inner world of soul and spirit.

The findings of these early 'scientists' was not conceived in intellectual form, as is the necessity today, but in imaginative, pictorial form. Theirs was not like the present world of theory and experiment, where hypotheses are tested, and solid proofs demonstrable in terms of weight, measure and number are arrived at by means of the five human senses and their extensions in the form of instruments of various kinds. Rather did they perceive the workings of the inner and outer worlds of human beings as deeds of the major and minor gods, nature spirits and so on. They used the only language they knew, which was that of what we now call mythology, and of legend, fairy story, fable, and parable—all of which appealed to the human imagination rather than the intellect, but which nevertheless ran little risk of being misconstrued or misunderstood. Much of the content of myth, legend and folk tale is of great interest to modern psychologists, who frequently discern in them echoes of ancient perspicacity and wisdom, symbolically and with creative imagination woven into the fabric of what at first sight appears to be 'mere' fiction. At long last the notion that our 'savage' forebears were lacking in intelligence is becoming increasingly accepted as a fallacy.

Oracles and Mystery cults

The oracle establishments had been preserved from the times of the catastrophe that marked the end of Atlantis at around 10,000 BC. The guardian of the Sun Oracle was Zarathustra or Zoroaster, who, according to Steiner, lived in much earlier times than the individual of the same name who lived in the sixth century BC. The original Zarathustra lived during the period of the ancient Persian civilization, which was thriving 5000–3000 BC, was known even after it declined. The historical Zarathustra divulged to his people that the exalted Sun or Light Spirit, otherwise known as Ahura Mazda or Ormuzd, would later descend to earth; this exalted Being was none other than the Christ. It is known that in Egypt during pre-Christian times, in the Ptolemaic-Roman period from 323 BC to AD 395, temple statues could be seen of the goddess Isis suckling her son Horus. This is unlikely to be mere coincidence, for the stories of Osiris incorporating the Mysteries of death, rebirth and resurrection were enacted by the priests and Pharaoh annually in the Mystery Plays at his temple in Abydos from as early as the twelfth dynasty (1991–1786 BC).

The following 2000 or so years saw the rise and fall of the Egypto-Chaldean civilization. The tradition of Osiris, his spouse Isis and their son Horus also incorporates the Mystery of death, rebirth and resurrection. In later centuries Christianity absorbed into itself certain elements of the cults which it could take over without doing violence to its already acknowledged practices and beliefs. The original purity of the spirituality and ethical integrity of those hierophants and their initiate associates was carefully preserved in the various Mystery Centres, which jealously guarded the secrets of the 'higher' unseen worlds.

In Chapter 2 was described how in the lower orders of the Mysteries, and among the common people, a ritual was performed whereby an image of the Sun-god was laid into a grave, and after three days would be taken up. This ceremony symbolized the death of the Sun-god and his restoration to life (see p. 57).

The Eleusinian Mysteries, which developed in the area of Athens, had at their centre rites and ceremonies that dramatized the death and decay of natural vegetation in the autumn and winter, which, however, was seen to be resurrected during the following spring. This they wove into the myth concerning Persephone (Proserpina to the Romans), who was carried off by Hades (Pluto), the brother of Zeus and King of the Underworld, who made her his Queen. She was sought by her grieving mother, Demeter (Ceres), goddess of agriculture, fertility and marriage, and, as a result of her impassioned pleas, Persephone was allowed to return to the world of light for six months of each year thereafter. It requires little imagination to interpret this particular legend, and others may equally well be analysed and seen to contain much in the way of factual information.

Very widespread indeed, and a strong rival to Christianity during the first three centuries of our era, was the Mystery religion that centred on Mithras, the god of light and guardian against evil, and who was often identified with the sun. This cult had its origin in Persia, and Mithras was usually represented as bestriding a bull, which he subsequently slays. From the dying creature issued the seed of life for the world, thus presenting the whole imagination as symbolical of regeneration.

Several Egyptian Mysteries centred on Osiris, a god who became ruler and judge of the underworld, and was the brother of and consort to Isis. He was killed by his brother, but his widow Isis, after a long search, found his body and revived it, after which he became the ruler of the dead. In this myth the periodical flooding of the Nile was the responsibility of Osiris, and the inferences concerning death and resurrection are easy to detect. Various sects were associated with Orpheus, who was such a skilled poet and musician that he was able to charm both man and beast. Members of these sects adopted as a main tenet of their religion one that was widely held by the Greeks at that time, namely, that matter and flesh constituted a positive evil, and that the soul, being spiritual and pure, should not be contaminated by matter. They believed that souls were subject to continual re-embodiment until they had advanced sufficiently as not to be required to be incarnated again.

Another school that looked upon the body as evil and the spirit as good was that which promulgated the teachings of Hermes Trismegistus. Their substance was highly ethical in character, for in addition to abstaining from the pleasures of the flesh they renounced such vices as malice, deceit, anger and avarice. The founder of this sect belonged to those who claimed to possess a secret *gnosis* (Greek, 'knowledge') whose system of cosmology and angelology was repugnant to the early Christian Church, which opposed all Gnostic teachings with vigour, partly because the Gnostics held that people could bring about their own salvation by their own efforts. Writings such as the Pistis-Sophia contain their main tenets and ideas, and many scholars consider it as something of a mystery as to why the Gnostic teachings faded as they did so quickly after the establishment of the early Christian Church.

The ancient Greek philosophies as represented by the Pythagoreans, Stoics, Platonists, Cynics and Peripatetics, who carried on the traditions of Aristotle, were all extant during the times we are dealing with, and although they were not without their influence—from the Platonists in particular—this is scarcely the place for their appraisal. Suffice it to say that it was at this time in history that individuals began to think for themselves, and to construct the very laws of thought itself in terms of logic and philosophy. The days of divine guidance and divine revelation, dependence upon oracles and suchlike had drawn to a close, as a kind of signal from the gods that humanity was now ready to become self-dependent and self-reliant. Such a severance from divine influences was bound to lead to a greater concentration on the secular and material, and history has shown this to be the case.

Christianity as Mystery

The origins of Christianity as generally understood are not traceable with any degree of accuracy, for the whole matter is shrouded in mystery. However, it is generally agreed that its basic practices and tenets involving ritual washings, the worship of a dying and rising god, and the certainty of eternal life through union (or reunion) with God have their origins in Gnosticism and the eastern Mystery Schools, with their traditions of secrecy and systems of initiation. Rudolf Steiner, for example, goes into considerable detail concerning the origins of the mass (see *The Christian Mystery*). Similarly, in his book *Christianity as Mystical Fact* he expands on the many issues involved.

Interesting in respect of this is the common and widespread

use throughout the New Testament of the appellation 'Lord' (Greek, *kyrios*) for Jesus, a term often employed in the Mystery Centres for a god or god-hero. Similarly, the name given to Jesus (*Iesous*) derives from the Hebrew word for 'saviour' (*yasha*), and this fits in neatly with the notions of redemption held by pre-Christian Gnostic Mystery cults. It is certain that notions of a pre-existent Christ, identified as the Creative Word (*Logos*), were rooted in the Mystery Schools, and this tenet also is seen to be warranted.

The constant hope and intention of initiates in the Mysteries was the birth of their higher self from their lower. This was called the festival of the inner Christ. Such an awakening can be achieved in modern times by dint of spiritual training. It actually is the case that what was revealed to the Mystery-pupils at Ephesus concerning the primeval Word was virtually that which led to the opening sentences of the Gospel of John, who was no stranger there. Such individuals were assured that the awakening of the Christ within them will be achieved, as a kind of 'Christmas', because the light will shine within them in a reversal of the imagery in John's Gospel: 'and the light will be comprehended in the darkness'. This is the underlying reason for holding Christmas services at midnight on the longest night of the year—the winter solstice, when all outside the church is dark.

Steiner asserted that this transformation was portrayed in the Mysteries. The great Christian event was a repetition in the physical world of what happened in the Mystery Schools: in the lesser Mysteries in the form of pictures, and in the greater Mysteries within human beings themselves. He maintained that everywhere in the inner sanctuaries of Egypt, in the Eleusian Mysteries and the Orphic cult of Greece, in the Near East among the Babylonians and Chaldeans, in the

Mithras cult of the Persians, and the Mysteries of the Ancient Indians, the holy night was celebrated in the same way. What was presented was a prophetic indication of the birth of Christ in the human being as an achievable result.

It is therefore no coincidence that the 'birth of the historical Jesus' was scheduled to take place at the winter solstice, when the planetary sun is weakest and there are more hours of darkness than of light. However, this notion is a mistake, for the birth being celebrated is really that of Christ in the human soul, not that of Jesus of Nazareth. For us human beings it is during the winter, when the earth itself is cold and bare, that the earth is awake, and conditions are most propitious for sinking as it were into our inner selves. In direct counterpoise to this state is the summer solstice, when it is commonly considered that the earth is most active and wide-awake, when outer nature is at is most colourful and abundant in leaf and flower. Steiner, however, insisted that the very opposite is true, expressing these contrasting moods in the following meditational verse:

Asleep is the soul of Earth
In Summer's heat,
While the Sun's outward glory
Rays through the realms of space.
Awake is the soul of Earth
In Winter's cold,
While the Sun's inmost being
Lightens in spirit.
Summer's day of joy
For Earth is sleep.
Winter's holy night
For Earth is day.

The message of Christ Jesus when he came down to earth was that of *equality,* for everyone has within him or her the divine 'seed' and can of themselves bring this seed to fruition provided they make the necessary effort; in other words, the former distinction between the Children of Men and the Children of God would no longer obtain. It is on account of his mission to the earth and its peoples that there is an approach by way of a spiritual path *directly* through him as the Way, the Truth and the Life (John 14:6; 1:14; 1:4 respectively) to God himself. In the Gospels Christ Jesus is on some occasions referred to as the Son of God and at others the Son of Man, in acknowledgement of his dual nature, but in actuality such terms are commonly regarded as inter-changeable.

Through Christianity, the self-transforming Logos was led away from separate personalities and focused on the unique personality of Jesus of Nazareth. That which had previously been distributed throughout the world was now brought together in a single personality. Jesus of Nazareth became the unique God-Man. In Jesus there was present once and for all something which must appear to man as the greatest of ideals, by which, in the course of repeated earth lives, he ought to unite himself more and more closely. Jesus took upon himself the task of raising all humanity. On the one hand, Christian convictions were presented in the form of Mystery truths; on the other, Mystery wisdom was clothed in Christian termi-nology. In spite of the protests of some believers in orthodox standpoints, it may be confidently reasoned that Christianity did actually grow out of the Mysteries.

However, it must be said that the Mystery Schools were also religious centres that provided guidance for the masses as and when needed. In *The Christian Mystery*, Rudolf Steiner explains just how closely dependent the newly popularized cults of the early Church were on the esoteric knowledge and practices that were released by the initiates at the time. Gnosticism in general was in any case itself very leaky, hence the proliferation of 'gospels' and other texts of similar sort, which ranged from the incredibly outrageous to the inconceivably boring. Furthermore, the endless arguing and disagreements among the Christian cognoscenti of the first half dozen or so centuries AD are for the most part little known by fundamentalist and certain evangelical sects. Their dogmas and other beliefs do not always possess the substantiality they imagine. In fact, 'God's word' was all too often the product of mental strife and heated argument, later to be followed by sectarianism and conflict, as history records.

Strangely enough—but perhaps not so strange—Rudolf Steiner presents us with the notion of 'myth' becoming manifest fact. Jesus of Nazareth was as historical as we can make him in an earthly sense; he was a man and a product of terrestrial history. Steiner was able to show that 'the Christ' was an exalted spiritual being with a cosmic history, and how the heavenly and earthly came together in the form of Christ Jesus. Thus myth became fact, as Steiner reveals in his aptly entitled book *Christianity as Mystical Fact*.

With the rise of Christianity came the demise of the Mystery Centres, and the reason for this is that they had outlived their usefulness, having served their purpose. This is especially so, perhaps, in the case of those Mystery Schools in which the sun figured large. This should not be surprising, for as mentioned earlier, the Christ was commonly associated with the sun. With his 'arrival' on earth as signified by his Incarnation it was to be expected that most of the Sun Mysteries would disappear, and this is what happened.

However, such esoteric schools should not to be confused with the many exoteric solar cults which comprised mere sun-worshippers, with their emphasis on the importance of the sun in the rhythms of nature as manifested in the daily round, the seasons, the sowing and harvesting of crops, and so on. By about 800 BC, during the fourth post-Atlantean epoch, the general acceptance of reincarnation and karma had died out in the western world, and it is only now that the twin tenets are being taken seriously. It is no coincidence that during this time-span such notions faded away, and that during this interlude the Christ Event occurred—during a kind of winter solstice for mankind as a whole. It was generally accepted that Christ incarnated on the earth once and once only; therefore, so ran the contention, we humans also visit the earth only once. Certainly the mutually supportive doctrines of self-created destiny and serial re-embodiment are difficult to the point of impossibility to arrive at by ordinary thinking processes. Significantly, Steiner regarded it as part of his mission to reintroduce these twin concepts in our own time, but with supporting confirmation supplied by spiritual science, thus going beyond mere standards of customary belief and disbelief.

He consistently showed that the Mysteries had served their purpose, and that henceforth their wisdom should be made available to everyone. He explained how the secrets of their schools were, in a very real sense, enacted on the stage of human history, and were relevant to contemporary circumstances. Christ Jesus, as an exalted spiritual Being, was the central figure in the whole drama. In fact, the events involving him and his mission made it plain that they concerned the inhabitants of the spiritual world as well as the terrestrial world. As spirit is indestructible, all members of the spiritual

Hierarchies ranking above our own have not experienced what we know as death. Part of the mission of the Christ Being on earth was to experience death on their behalf, and this is perhaps the greatest Mystery of all.

The scholar Robert Reitzenstein (1861–1931), in his book *The Hellenistic Mystery-religions*, offered three important conclusions concerning New Testament study: first, it is certain that Greek and near-eastern religions exercised a profound influence on the theology of the New Testament, especially on that of Paul; second, that the early Church's declarations and cult were based on the Mystery religions and Gnosticism; and third, that early Christianity's notion of redemption by the death and resurrection accorded with pre-Christian Mystery wisdom. Such an august authority as *Peake's Commentary on the Bible* (623b) declares: 'There is no doubt that Paul used the language of the Mysteries, and, in spite of the fears and suspicions of modern thinkers, actually validated their reality by associating them with Christianity, not the obverse, namely the dread notion that the new religion was actually—but altogether properly—deeply rooted in the Mysteries.'

Such nervously desperate attempts on the part of modern biblical scholars to denigrate the Mysteries serve only to weaken their case. A further example of the wobbly standpoint of the established Christian Churches is that Christianity began just under two thousand years ago, but this depends on dubious premises. In what is widely acknowledged as a standard work, Dr J.W.C. Wand, *A History of the Early Church to AD 500,* appears the following:

In a period of doubt and disorganization (the Mystery cults) offered a guarantee of salvation and immortality. By their secrecy and their elaborate ceremonies they appealed to the love of esoteric knowledge in those who had no power to follow philosophic reasoning. It is often alleged that Christianity borrowed from them some of their most distinctive features, such as a belief in a Saviour God and the use of sacraments. While that is manifestly untrue, it is very likely that Christian leaders often worked out their own systems from against the background of the Mysteries and in forms of thought that were common to both. The similarity between the terminology of the early Christian writings and that of the Mysteries shows how great was at once the danger and the triumph of the Church. Christianity beat the Mysteries on their own ground. It had the advantage of being based not on a myth but on a historic Person. It appealed equally to the individual and to the whole human race.

Matters were not so 'untrue' as Dr Wand would have us believe, however. There can be no doubting of the man on the spot, namely Paul, who parallels the opening verses of John's Gospel in his letter to the Colossians (1:15–17) with references to God's 'own dear Son ... Who is the image of the invisible God, the firstborn of every creature; for by him were all things created, that are in heaven, and that are in earth, visible and invisible, whether they be thrones, or dominions, or principalities, or powers: all things were created by him and for him: and he is before all things, and by him all things consist.' Whereas Christian 'open Mysteries' were revelations to be published abroad (I Corinthians 15:51; Colossians 1:26 f; Ephesians 1:9; 3:3). The truths of God, the real Mysteries, were always hidden from the masses and subject to interpretation only by those 'in the know'. As for the spiritual

Hierarchies, some modern theologians consider these rather presumptuously as 'the non-human, angelic or demonic powers' thought of as peopling the universe and controlling the planets. 'If Paul shared with the false teachers this type of astrological superstition (which he did), he did not share one grain of the fear of, or attempts to propitiate, these sinister forces' (*Peake's Commentary on the Bible*, 385b). One might be forgiven for retorting that such imperiously emotive language is not only unwarranted but also inaccurate.

Paul does not hesitate to speak (Colossians 2:2) of 'the acknowledgement of the mystery of God, and of the Father, and of Christ', and in I Corinthians 2:7 of 'the wisdom of God in a mystery, even the hidden wisdom, which God ordained before the world unto our glory'. He also reminded those early Christians of the necessary ethical standards demanded: 'Let a man so account of us, as of the ministers of Christ, and stewards of the mysteries of God, that a man be found faithful' (I Corinthians 4:1–2). (Perhaps the first letter of the most significant Mystery in the earth's history should have been in upper case.)

Non-Christian attestations

It bears repetition that the Christ Being was the only member of the 'hosts of heaven' to experience death as human beings do. His death on the cross was therefore unique in that it served heavenly as well as earthly beings and their purposes in terms of evolution of both humanity and the earth upon which its members dwelt. The ritual enacting the symbolic death and resurrection of initiates of the highest order immediately below that of 'Father', namely 'Sun-man or Sun-hero', took place in circumstances of the highest secrecy. By contrast, the actual death and resurrection of Christ Jesus took place before the very eyes of the world—in public. In this connection it may come as something of a surprise to find that this viewpoint is precisely that to be found in contemporary Judaism. The following extract from the first page of Jewish scholar Gershom Scholem's book *The Messianic Idea in Judaism* (Schoken Books, 1971) reads:

A totally different concept of redemption determines the attitude to Messianism in Judaism and in Christianity; what appears to the one as a proud indication of its understanding and a positive achievement of its message is most unequivocally belittled and disputed by the other. Judaism, in all its forms and manifestations, has always maintained a concept of redemption *as an event which takes place publicly, on the stage of history* and within the community. It is an occurrence which takes place in the visible world which cannot be conceived apart from such a visible appearance. In contrast, Christianity conceives of redemption as *an event in the spiritual and unseen realm*, an event which is reflected in the soul, in the private world of each individual, and which effects an inner transformation which need not correspond to anything outside. [My italics]

In view of this assertion, may it not rather be the case that the matter is not one of either/or but of both/and? Christ appeared in human form, which had been prepared by the Hebrews—the chosen people—as the exalted paragon of earthly man. All Mystery wisdom had therefore to assume a new form. Previously, this wisdom existed exclusively in order to enable human beings to bring themselves to the appropriate state of soul that renders them capable of recognizing the Christ who had become human, and from this centre of all wisdom to understand the entire natural and spiritual worlds. The whole Christ Event, therefore, not only constituted and marked the centre of human physical evolution, but it was also the centre of the entire universe to which humanity belongs. After his crucifixion and resurrection, Christ came to dwell in the world into which human beings pass after death. Thus the realm known to the Greeks as Hades, 'the kingdom of the shades', and to the Hebrews as Sheol was to be illuminated by the 'Light of the World'.

In effect, therefore, those individuals who were capable of comprehending the Mysteries attending the Christ Event were able to take with them what they had acquired by dint of their experiences in the world of the senses into the spiritual world. Hence, by virtue of the processes of reincarnation, souls were enabled to bring back to the earthly world what the Christ Impulse had become for them during their sojourn in the spiritual worlds between death and rebirth. It may be seen, therefore, that, seedlike, the power inherent in this impulse has been able to grow, however slowly, into the whole processes of human evolution. It is reasonable to contend that Christianity in all its manifestations is still only at an embryonic stage. Its rate of progress has been, is and will be wholly dependent on the capacity for succeeding generations to assimilate what they may of its main purpose, namely, the ideal and practice of a truly universal brotherhood. Christ was, by God, 'predestined to be conformed to the image of his Son, that he might be the firstborn among many brethren' (Romans 8:29).

It is noteworthy that Rudolf Steiner made the following italicized statement almost word for word. In his book *Christianity as Mystical Fact* he explained how the secrets of the Mystery Schools were, in a very real sense, *enacted on the stage of human history*, and would be revealed as actual and relevant to contemporary circumstances. Christ Jesus, as an exalted spiritual Being, was the central figure in the whole drama. In fact, the events involving him and his mission made it plain that they concerned the inhabitants of the spiritual world as well as the terrestrial world. It may seem remarkable that Scholem and Steiner agree on this, though it must be clearly borne in mind that Steiner's standpoint was not that of orthodox Christian belief.

Most confessed Christians, although they acknowledge all the occurrences referred to earlier as 'the Christ Event', are content to experience them and their implications for their own inner life rather than the actuality of the incidents in Palestine. It is difficult for the modern mind to achieve a little more than regarding them symbolically rather than as actual happenings. Nonetheless, it is true that no incident occurs in the material world without its corresponding effects in the spiritual world, and vice versa, and this aspect is not widely appreciated.

One of the main purposes of the so-called Christ Event, namely the incarnation, crucifixion and resurrection of the Messiah, was the redemption of the whole of humanity, as 'he was the true Light that lighteth every man that cometh into the world. He was in the world, and the world was made by him, and the world knew him not. He came unto his own, and his own received him not' (John 1:9–11). It is debatable whether John foresaw that the new era was due to pass through the kind of 'Dark Age' for as long as two millennia before resurgence would take place. John declares that the Light of the World would not shine in the immediate future, but only later, when orthodox Christianity, devoid of spiri-

tuality as it had become, would become truly spiritualized—
and that time is now.

Once again, Gershom Scholem's ideas fit neatly into the
foregoing discussion:

> In the Zohar ... the author expresses his vision in the
> imagery of the Tree of Life and the Tree of Knowledge
> (from which death depends). Since Adam sinned, the world
> has been governed not by the Tree of Life (as it properly
> should be) but by the Tree of Knowledge. The Tree of Life
> is entirely and exclusively holy, with no admixture of evil,
> no adulteration or impurity or death or limitation. The
> Tree of Knowledge, on the other hand, contains both good
> and evil, purity and impurity, virtue and vice, and therefore
> under its rule there are things forbidden and things per-
> mitted, things fit for consumption and things unfit, the
> clean and the unclean. In an unredeemed world the Torah
> is revealed in positive and negative commandments and all
> that these imply, but in the redeemed future uncleanliness
> and unfitness and death will be abolished. In an unre-
> deemed world the Torah must be interpreted in manifold
> ways—literal, allegorical, mystical; but in the redeemed
> future it will be revealed in the pure spirituality of the Tree
> of Life, without the 'clothing' it put on after Adam sinned.
> It will be wholly inward, entirely holy.

It takes little imagination to recognize the Luke Jesus as
representing the Tree of Life, and the Matthew boy as the
Tree of Knowledge. Christ Jesus himself declares that he is
'the way, the truth, and the life' (John 14:6). And John's
Gospel states (1:4) that 'in him was life; and the life was the
light of mankind'. Therefore, with reference to Scholem's
viewpoint we can gather that the redeemer was representative

of both Life and Knowledge, salient attributes which Christ Jesus acquired from the Luke and Matthew Jesuses respectively. We all inherited our corruptible body from the first Adam-ancestor, with 'continuous deaths' in prospect in the form of successive earthly re-embodiments stretching into the future. It is therefore highly significant that Adam's expulsion from the Garden of Eden took place, for by his disobedience he had to be denied access to the Tree of Life (Genesis 3:22–4).

However, our second Adam-ancestor, himself incorruptible and indestructible, is capable of bestowing this factor of resurrection on those individuals who accept him into themselves. The Word as life-giver in the shape of the pre-existent Christ has the power to restore the pre-expulsion status quo according to John the Evangelist: 'But as many as received him, to them gave he the power to become sons of God, even to them who believe on his name' (1:12). The certainty of 'those who accept' to be redeemed is thus made clear; but what is also made plain is that such 'acceptance' and the bestowal of 'sonship' must be an act of free will on the part of each individual person.

Just as Adam's fateful step had been from a state of sinlessness and spiritual bondage to earthly freedom of choice and consequently a state of sin, so the act taken to parallel it, taken by the Messiah in perfect freedom, was instrumental in facilitating every possibility of man's reversal of that step. The fact of Christ's taking on of the completely human condition with the exception of sin, and consequent inevitable death, is central to the notion of redemption. It was necessary that this occur, and this is why Christ was not, in the days of the apostolic Church, recognized as the Son of God until his resurrection. This signified that Christ had overcome death, thereby making it possible for man to do likewise.

These factors validate the death and resurrection of Christ Jesus, which had to take place in actuality, in reality, in the material world, as enacted symbolically in the Mystery Schools, which fully anticipated these events. They also undermine the widely held notion of Christianity as primarily a body of teaching, and the biblical Scriptures as a primary source of moral standards for everyday life. It is often over-looked, even though evidence to the contrary is glaringly obvious, that Christianity is based on a deed, namely, that of redemption of all sinners. The whole affair is unique in that, to put it simply, it is an example of the interference of spiritual beings in earthly affairs. It must be remembered that an important feature of Christ's mission was to 'take away the sin of the world' (John 1:21). As has been mentioned many times, that particular 'sin' (not sins, as often understood) is human egotism in all its forms. By his supreme act of self-sacrifice, he gave us an example of its main motivation—a matchless capacity for love.

Christ and the Sun Mysteries

In the teachings emanating from the Mystery Schools the sun, and the light that radiated from it, figured as supremely important. In fact, it was worshipped, revered and esteemed, not as a ball of fire in the heavens which made life itself possible on earth, but rather as the home of an exalted Sun Being. The neophytes in the Mysteries were told that spiritual as well as ordinary light streamed from the sun, and that this stream, vitalized by the Sun Being himself, took them beyond death into the spiritual worlds, and accompanied them until, eventually, they would return to the earth. They felt and were conscious that it was the Spirit of the Sun that gave them immortality. All this infers that to them reincarnation was an actuality, and not a dubious notion as many look on it today.

With regard to the Sun Mysteries of western tradition, there were seven stages within the initiation process: (1) Raven; (2) Occultist or Listener; (3) Defender (of the Spirit); (4) Sphinx; (5) Spirit of the People (e.g. Persian, Greek, Israelite); (6) Sun Man, and (7) Father. As might be expected, the neophytes were sworn to secrecy on pain of death, although there were the inevitable leakages of various details of the secret teachings, which were inevitably subject to garbling and misrepresentation. Rudolf Steiner, in *Christianity and the Mysteries of Antiquity*, states that those who held the highest office in the Mystery Schools or Centres were called 'Fathers', an echo of which custom exists today. These Fathers, who were able to communicate with the gods and other spiritual beings, were the teachers within the Mystery Schools, and were known as 'Sons (or Children) of God'. Their pupils and neophytes, being of lower status, were known as 'Children (or Sons) of Man'.

The notion or concept of God himself as *Father* comes directly from the Mysteries. As might be imagined, there was no need for the Christ himself to undergo initiation, for he was the mighty Sun-god, who sacrificed himself not only for the benefit of human beings but also for the gods themselves. It is perfectly natural for anthropomorphisms to have been employed, as exemplified by the reference to the All-encompassing World Spirit as 'Father', and the exalted spiritual Being belonging to the Second Hierarchy, namely the *Exousiai* or Spirits of Form (Authorities or Powers), as 'Son'.

As indicated earlier, the sun was regarded as the home of

exalted spiritual Beings, and it figures large in the image-rich language of the time. With all its connotations of light, the giver of life and the central focus of the world, as well as its evident power and importance, the sun was assured a position and significance in religious terms far higher than it holds today, New Age movement adherents, pantheists and such-like notwithstanding. It is certain that hidden in those Mystery Centres was the knowledge that a spiritual Being of an exalted nature was in the process of descending to the earth in order to accomplish a mission of both earthly and cosmic importance.

It is utterly reasonable that this knowledge, leaking out and being taken up in various forms by those cults and Mystery Schools that have been mentioned (and there were many others) gave rise to all the confusion and misunderstanding concerning the sun, as representative of the Christ himself. In many minds he was identified with the sun; hence all the confusion concerning the winter solstice as marking the 'rebirth' of the material sun with the birth of Jesus of Nazareth and also with the 'birth' or incarnation of the Christ in this individuality at his baptism in the River Jordan. Here we are reminded of the Sol Invictus, the victory of the sun over winter. The 'Spiritual Sun' as Christ entered the cosmic winter solstice at the turning point of time is another reference to Mystery wisdom being enacted on the stage of the earth.

In the first chapter of John's Gospel (1:9) we are reminded of the enormous significance of light: (The Word) 'was the true Light, which lighteth every man that cometh into the world.' The priests of the Mystery Schools taught that ordinary sunlight was the outer revelation of the Sun-god himself, and that although the sun set over the horizon, it did not die but was certain to rise again, thus signifying his eternal nature. The counterpart of light is of course darkness, and these two factors are experienced by most life-forms on the earth in truly archetypal fashion. The phenomenon of day and night, and the regularity of their alternation, and indeed opposition in nature and manifestation is so common and ordinary that they are easily overlooked. However, these two principles utterly dominated the thinking of all civilizations during the millennium immediately preceding the Christ Event.

This practice and its symbolism was absorbed by the people at various levels of understanding, and it was traditional to enact the whole rite at the time of the winter solstice, when the path of the planetary sun runs lowest in the sky, when the days were at their shortest and the nights were darkest and longest. Such ceremonies were observed by many communities even after their true meaning and significance had been forgotten. A close parallel is the traditional midnight mass still celebrated in Roman Catholic churches, symbolically at the turn of the day, when the building is darkened and the altar brightly lit. Thus light and darkness were employed as powerful tokens of the 'True Light' and the overcoming of Darkness and all that this conveyed.

It was known to the initiated priests within the Mysteries that the sublime Sun-god of whom they spoke was the same Being who in due time would be acknowledged as the Christ. However, this could only be when he was incarnated in the physical body of Jesus of Nazareth at his baptism by John in the River Jordan. In a very real sense the Christ as Sun-god, having appeared on earth, could not be present in the sun. It was his mission to unite himself with the earth and its human inhabitants: 'Lo, I am with you always, even unto the end of the age' (Matthew 28:20). The inference is plain in his declaration that his kingdom was not of this world (John 18:36) but that he had come from other, cosmic or heavenly realms. In other words, he was of divine and not human nature, and this is why, as all Adoptionists understand, he was obliged while on earth to avail himself of the 'perfect' human body that Jesus of Nazareth provided for him. His ascension was into the heavenly realms, in this case the etheric world.

Paul's strange conversion threw the Jewish community into confusion and bewilderment, and they plotted to kill him, but he escaped by being let down the city walls in a basket. Rudolf Steiner averred that Paul was a pupil of initiates in the Mysteries, and that his firm conviction that the sublime Sun Being was to be found only in the heavenly world led to him being an enthusiastic opponent of the new Christianity. With his Damascus experience, Paul realized he had encountered Christ, whom he also knew as the Sun Being on the earthly plane. The shock was so great that he was sightless for three days. When he had recovered with the help of Ananias he was firmly convinced that the man Jesus was indeed the Christ-bearer, and that this same Being was the Sun Being of Mystery teachings who had now united himself with the earth. From being the new religion's most enthusiastic opponent he became its most dedicated proponent and missionary. He came to realize that had the Christ not appeared on the earth, but remained as the Sun-god only, humankind would have deteriorated in every way. In him Paul recognized the long-awaited Redeemer, whose gift of true enlightenment was now available.

By way of digression, it must be said that if the whole Christ Event—his descent into a long-prepared physical body provided by Jesus of Nazareth, his crucifixion and resurrection—had not occurred, humanity would have come to believe that everything in and on the surrounding cosmos is solely material in nature and constitution. This state of affairs is rapidly developing in present times. Naturalists, conservationists and ecologists all agree that our planet is in grave danger of becoming utterly barren and unable to sustain the living organisms that it now supports, including human beings themselves. Steiner confirmed that it is perfectly possible for the earth to abandon its mission if the current rate of human exploitation of its resources continues at the present rate. The absurd attitude that still exists that it is somehow the privilege of mankind to 'conquer' nature instead of to cooperate with it is leading us closer and closer to disasters of many and diverse kinds.

In general, we respect those individuals and teams of investigators who extend their knowledge in all fields of human endeavour for the common good, but they are being thwarted by out-and-out materialists, who in turn foster attitudes of mind that gives rise within society to self-seeking, greed and exploitation of people and resources. The cultivation of the trivial and the superficial is now widespread, and more and more opportunities are provided for folk to 'enjoy themselves', take things easy and live a life of leisure. The proliferation of local and national lotteries, entertaining competitions with money or material goods or exotic holidays as prizes, and competitiveness in sport and so on are fundamentally demoralizing for the individual and corrodes society.

Set against such essentially degrading practices and pastimes are those who make room in their daily lives for matters of a spiritual nature, and that have a charitable and altruistic character. Unfortunately, many people who turn to organized religion for encouragement and support find themselves decoyed into activities that degenerate into routines, with little prospect of advancement. Others try to enliven things by combining their serious goals with trivialities or extravagances of emotion or affectation. In short, it is a matter of each to their own wish and will.

Christian initiation

Rudolf Steiner, in the book *The Christian Mystery*, maintained that John's Gospel was representative, in many and profound ways, of the path of Christian initiation. He described the seven 'stations' as significant experiences that might be expected by those who faithfully and earnestly applied themselves to their seven stages of advancement. These are:

1. *Washing of the Feet* (John 13:3–15). In Christian tradition humility is a significant virtue, for as John Bunyan's shepherd boy in *The Pilgrim's Progress* observed:

> He that is down, needs fear no fall
> He that is low, no Pride:
> He that is humble, ever shall
> Have God to be his Guide.

It is probably no coincidence that he chose this expression, for it echoes the 'Fall' of mankind generally. Steiner pointed out that all categories of living beings, including the divine Hierarchies, are dependent in various ways on those who rank below them. For example, the earth beneath our feet is the first stage in a process which enables us to maintain our material body—the plants take up what is provided by the mineral kingdom, and the animals and ourselves rely on the plants for daily nourishment. Similarly, the ambrosia on which the gods were said to depend is none other than human love. Deuteronomy 6:5 is emphatic: 'love thy God with all thy heart, with all thy soul, and with all thy might'. The only commandment of Christ Jesus himself is: 'love one another as I have loved you' (John 12:15, 17). Rather than disdaining the lower orders of Creation therefore, we should be grateful to them. By practising the greatest intensity of feeling in these regards, aspirers to higher knowledge actually experience the sensation of water washing over their feet.

2. *The Scourging* (John 19:1). This stage is characterized by vivid pictures and impressions of the Christ being mercilessly flogged, and the pains he was made to bear. In similar fashion the aspirer must needs suffer—and steadfastly endure—'the slings and arrows of outrageous fortune' to an enhanced degree, as well as feelings of being cruelly beaten up.

3. *The Crown of Thorns* (John 19:2). Many people who 'believe' in, for example, homoeopathic medicine, the bio-dynamic philosophy and other organic methods of agri-culture, the 'doctrines' of reincarnation and karma, and have somewhat strange notions concerning education are often regarded as 'weirdos' and cranks. Carrying on regardless in spite of being labelled as such is the lot of those who fly in the face of orthodoxy. The attempts of the neophyte at clear and sustained envisioning of images and sharing the feelings of derision and ridicule which the Christ also experienced may become aware of a prickling sensation of the scalp, perhaps accompanied by severe headache.

4. *The Crucifixion* (John 19:16–18). This stage represents considerable advancement, and may well be somewhat unnerving, at least to start with. This exercise involves making

earnest, even strenuous, efforts to experience the feeling that
the physical body is somehow foreign to the real Self. One of
the responses of those seeing a corpse for the first time is that it
is utterly stiff and motionless. It is a mere object that does
not—cannot—make any kind of response, and this can be
extremely shocking. The earnest efforts to relive in the imagination the unspeakable pain and suffering which attended
the crucifixion, that fervent contemplation of it, results in the
appearance of the stigmata—the bleeding from the palms of
both hands and perhaps also the right side of the chest.

5. *The 'Mystic Death'*. Just as, at the moment of actual death,
we are, in an instant, deprived of our sense-organs and the
power of movement, so the aspiring candidate is called upon
to imagine, with the greatest intensity, how this must feel.
Everything goes dark, and the aspirant experiences the terror
that comes with the sensation of the presence of unutterable
evil. This is traditionally described as the descent into hell.
The time comes, however, when, as if a dark curtain is rent
from top to bottom, the light which illuminates the spiritual
world appears.

6. *The Resurrection* (John 11:24, 25). After experiencing the
terrors of being buried in the darkness of earth, the neophyte
feels great relief and release. Gradually he is made aware of an
expansion of consciousness, which extends to the far reaches
of the cosmos, and its secrets are revealed.

7. *The Ascension* (John 20:17). This experience is inexpres-
sibly sublime. By tradition the heavens are above us, and
ascension into them may be characterized as veritable union
with the Divine.

These seven stages have a sound ancestry, and the manifold
literature and traditions attaching to them clearly indicate

that their origins are firmly rooted in Mystery teachings. The 'ascents' tradition of 'ascending via the Holy Spirit to the higher spheres' was well known to the Kabbalists, as might be expected, as well as to the Gnostics, who also reckoned on seven stages or degrees of ascent. The so-called 'Songs of degrees' represented by Psalms 120 to 134 are widely acknowledged to be 'ascent' literature. Paul knew about the mysticism of heaven ascents, as hinted in his report in II Corinthians 12:2 of knowing a man who was 'caught up to the third heaven'. Notable, too, are the traditions of James conducting discourses on the 'steps of the temple', and their mention in the Cairo Damascus Document.

Modern mysteries are material

It is regrettable that present and ongoing ideas and attitudes alienate us from the cosmos. Public interest in astrology and astronomy is growing rapidly; everyone seems to be fascinated by 'space', but it is very much a case of the blind leading the blind. There is much empty talk about 'outer space', from which, according to some 'experts', we came—but ignoring the fact that we are already *there* as well as *here*. The obsession of modern science with the question as to whether or not there is life on planets other than our own is symptomatic of its narrow and fragmented approach. Of course there is 'life' on other planets—but not necessarily the kind of 'life' we as human beings are experiencing. It does not allow for anything that is supersensory, yet at a stroke it is dismissing the concept, which after all is not too difficult to arrive at, that the whole universe may be teeming with kinds of 'life' of which they cannot possibly conceive, simply because they cannot *perceive* them.

Today's chief oracle, in the shape of television, spews out daily helpings of mock-phantasy programmes in which characters with magical powers are presented as reality. Nowadays viewers are fed on a rich diet of crime, violence and murder, all in the name of entertainment. Is it so odd that the fundamental Mystery rites, wherever they were represented and observed by the various peoples of the world, are without exception concerned with *death?* Human as well as animal sacrifice was common practice in times long past, and many modern anthropologists and historians usually regard such a custom as repulsively inhuman, cruel, disgusting and reprehensible. However, the motives of the priests and others concerned—even quite often the 'victims' themselves—were, in their seemingly strange ceremonies, merely conforming to the mores of their times, and should be judged accordingly. An important sacramental rite in the Mysteries consisted in showing the sacrifice of the god, the death of the god, and his resurrection after three days. This rite was a pointer to anyone who penetrated more deeply into the external world that death in this outer world may reveal that the true reality must be sought beyond death. Such a conviction may eventually replace the 'sure and certain hope' as peddled by a very uncertain Church of England.

The proper job of organized Christian religion is to promote spirit, but step by step throughout its history it has done away successively with spirit and soul and now people are left with a mechanistic view of the human being. That organized religion is failing is now widely acknowledged. History has shown all too clearly that the Church has not 'triumphed', as evidenced by its ever-emptying chapels and the headlong rush into materialism, hedonism, and national and international political and social chaos. The current 'New Age' crusade for the most part merely echoes smatterings of scrappy quasi-Gnostic ideas. There is little substance to any of them. Druids, bards, witches and warlocks, astrologers and psychics there are a-plenty, but their spiritual harvest is invariably sparse. As with the medieval mystics, they lacked the structure and discipline identifiable as scientific method. Science in all branches of technology is roaring ahead simply because it is seen to work. But spiritual science is equally as valid, as scientists would discover if they took seriously the fact that in all matter spirit is constantly at work.

4
THE TWO FAMILIES

Anyone who takes their stand on a mystical origin of the
Gospels can easily explain the inconsistencies, and will also
discern harmonies between the fourth Gospel and the others.
Rudolf Steiner, *Christianity as Mystical Fact*

Belief and actuality

Sometimes it becomes necessary, if truths are to be arrived at,
to think the unthinkable and conceive what might formerly
have been considered inconceivable. Where the Gospels are
concerned this kind of approach is essential. The bare stories
as they are need to be augmented by more factors than are
immediately apparent; otherwise, they would be as easy to
read and understand as the daily newspaper. The Gospels
themselves contain ample warning that they contain, as it
were, signs or clues that can only be understood by those with
ears to hear. This implies that those whose level of understanding is that of parable, allegory and the like have much to
learn.

If ingrained preconceptions are put aside, unbelief sus-
pended, and challenges taken up, unfamiliar notions and
perspectives, evidential material from hitherto untapped
sources will attract the consideration they deserve. Comparatively few Christian believers know that there were gospels galore of Gnostic and apocryphal origin which were
rejected as being dubious, spurious or unreliable, and—
mercifully—excluded from the canon. These gospels, some of

which are so fanciful as to bear scant if any credibility, range from the entertainingly quaint to the tedious. For the most part these books are unknown to, and almost certainly unread by, the majority of Christians, their existence being known almost exclusively to theologians and biblical scholars.

The canonical Gospels, however, are certainly capable of being understood on several levels other than the purely literal; indeed, contended Steiner, they were deliberately written with this provision in mind. Jesus himself gave the cue for this, which was, not unnaturally, taken up by his disciples. He gave warnings concerning them: 'And when he was alone, they that were about him with the twelve asked him of the parable (of the sower). And he said unto them, Unto you is given to know the mystery of the Kingdom of God; but unto them that are without, all these things are done in parables: That seeing they may see, and not perceive; and hearing they may hear, and not understand; lest at any time they should be converted, and their sins forgiven them' (Mark 4:10–12). It might seem that here the implication is that with conversion come responsibilities and commitments which may not be welcome to every aspirant.

Later in the same chapter (Mark 4:22–5) we read: 'For there is nothing hid, which shall not be manifested; neither has taken place any secret thing that does not come to light. If anyone has ears to hear, let him hear. And he said unto them, Take heed what ye hear; with what measure ye mete, it shall be measured to you: and unto you that hear more shall be given. For he that hath, to him shall be given: and he that hath not, from him shall be taken that which he hath.' For example, it would be unwise for such to approach the miracle stories with wide-eyed wonder, taking them to represent actual events. This would infer that certain laws of nature were broken; but science, whose very existence depends on such laws, must challenge such claims. However, once such miracle stories are elevated to the spiritual or 'mystical' level, namely, that which was intended, they make perfect sense— but only to those who are able to interpret them correctly. The obvious answer to this is to take seriously the biblical texts that clearly indicate that there were indeed two different boys, and the stubbornness of the Churches and their leaders in refusing to acknowledge this simple fact may be due as much to historical necessity as their own intransigence.

A common area of confusion is that of distinguishing the difference between the appellations Jesus and Christ, Jesus Christ and Christ Jesus, Son of Man and Son of God, Lord, King and so on, which has come about over the centuries. When, as a popular carol reads, 'Mary was that mother mild, Jesus Christ her little child', it is clearly exhibiting ignorance of the facts. Gradually, the name Jesus has become identical with Christ, thus giving the impression that he was born in the usual way, which was not the case. Christ never had a childhood, for it implies some kind of beginning, but 'before Abraham was, I am' (John 8:58).

The presence of two Jesuses are biblical 'truths', and this cannot be denied: both the Matthew Jesus and the Luke Jesus were human beings, whereas (the) Christ is a wholly spiritual being whose incursion into earthly affairs lasted a bare three years—from the time of his baptism in the River Jordan until his crucifixion. The genealogy of the Luke Jesus takes us right to up to God himself—yet he had an earthly father as well. By contrast, Matthew's genealogy ceases with Abraham—a human being only. When, throughout the Gospels, Jesus (the) Christ refers to his 'Father' he is certainly not referring to one that is mortal. John, in his Gospel makes mention of 'father' in lower case only once (4:53), which choice tells its own story. When Christ Jesus asked who his mother was (Matthew 12:48, Mark 3:33), his answer to his own question was certainly unexpected. Moreover, the 'mother' of his post-baptismal Gospel is never referred to as 'Mary', and why this is so is more interesting than most Christians realize.

Jesus of Nazareth was the offspring of the Luke Mary and Joseph, both of whom were declared suitable and proper to satisfy all requirements. Joseph's ancestry, fully registered, was therefore acceptable, and the Luke Mary, although her forebears are not listed, received her warrant from none other than the angel Gabriel at the event known as the Annunciation (Luke 1:26–35). She was therefore the chosen mother of the Jesus who, after being conjoined with the corporeal members of Zarathustra at the time of the incident in the temple in Jerusalem, was marked out as the adult Jesus of Nazareth. There is nothing to give the impression that it was the Christ Being who was incarnated. He was never a neonate as generally understood, for he was not actually born in the usual sense. As argued in Chapter 1, it was with his Adoption at the age of 30 that Jesus of Nazareth was declared by God to be his Son—an announcement that appears in all four Gospels on the occasion of his baptism.

The whole business of names, especially that meant to designate the Christ Being and the purely human Jesus, is difficult and ambiguous. At Matthew 2:4 the Greek *ho Christos* is translated as 'Christ' in most Bibles. However, this appellation means 'the anointed one', which in turn is a rendering of the Hebrew word *messia*. Furthermore, this word is often employed as a synonym for Jesus, especially nowadays, which adds more contention to an already grievous problem. It would seem that the safest guide to anything near accuracy might be to consider the usage of the many references to 'Sonship' of God. The employment together of the two words 'Priest' and 'King' is an indication that the bearers of such titles have been anointed and are therefore individuals who have been chosen or set apart and consecrated to the service of God. When, at Matthew 16:15–16, Jesus asks his disciples whom they thought he was, Simon Peter replied, 'Thou art the Christ, the Son of the living God,' which indeed he undoubtedly was.

Jesus of Bethlehem and Jesus of Nazareth

The genealogies of the Jesus at Matthew 1:1–17 and the Jesus at Luke 3:23–38 are totally different and wholly irreconcilable. The discrepancies are there in the Christian Scriptures, and cannot and must not be ignored in spite of widespread reluctance to do so by orthodox theologians. Not surprisingly, ingenious attempts to prove otherwise have for various reasons foundered, and the problems they pose are conveniently shelved. The evidence, it is claimed, is simply not there and, just as everything must be questioned, everything must—in these uncertain days—be proved. There are countless allusions and so-called 'proof-texts' in the Old Testament to events in the New Testament, and indeed many people wonder whether the citations to be found in the Old Testament books actually dictate what appears in the New. Certainly, the web of prophecy and fulfilment is very sure and very extensive, some of the connections between the two being extraordinarily detailed and complex. The two genealogies are here listed, in line of *descent*:

Matthew	Luke
1 *Abraham*	1 God
2 Isaac	2 Adam
3 Jacob	3 Seth
4 Judas	4 Enos
5 Perez	5 Cainan
6 Hezron	6 Mahahaleel
7 Aram	7 Jared
8 Aminadab	8 Enoch
9 Nahshon	9 Methuselah
10 Salmon	10 Lamech
11 Boaz	11 Noah
12 Obed	12 Shem
13 Jesse	13 Arphaxad
14 *David*	14 Cainan
15 *Solomon*	15 Shelah
16 Rehoboam	16 Eber
17 Abia	17 Peleg
18 Asa	18 Reu
19 Jehosaphat	19 Serug
20 Joram	20 Nahor
21 Uzziah	21 Terah
22 Jotham	22 *Abraham*
23 Ahaz	23 Isaac
24 Hezekia	24 Jacob
25 Mannaseh	25 Judah
26 Amon	26 Perez
27 Josiah	27 Hezron
28 Jeconiah	28 Aram
29 Shealtial	29 Aminadab
30 Zerubbabel	30 Nahshon
31 Abiud	31 Salmon

32 Zerubbabel	32 Boaz	55 Neri
33 Eliakim	33 Obed	56 Shealtiel
34 Azor	34 Jesse	57 Zerabbabel
35 Zadok	35 *David*	58 Rhesa
36 Achim	36 *Nathan*	59 Joanan
37 Eliud	37 Mattatha	60 Joda
38 Eleazar	38 Menna	61 Josech
39 Matthan	39 Melea	62 Semein
40 Jacob	40 Eliakim	63 Mattathias
41 *Joseph*	41 Jonam	64 Maath
42 (*Christ*)	42 Joseph	65 Naggai
	43 Judas	66 Esli
	44 Symeon	67 Nahum
	45 Levi	68 Amos
	46 Matthat	69 Mattathias
	47 Jorim	70 Joseph
	48 Eliezer	71 Jannai
	49 Jesus	72 Melchi
	50 Er	73 Levi
	51 Elmadam	74 Matthat
	52 Cosam	75 Heli
	53 Addi	76 *Joseph*
	54 Melchi	77 *Jesus*

The two pedigrees established

On the authority of the two genealogies listed in Matthew and Luke there were two Jesus boys, and two sets of parents both called Joseph and Mary—a common enough coincidence in view of the popularity of such names at the time. Both Jesuses shared David as a common ancestor, as the genealogies in Matthew and Luke substantiate. David's status is established

(I Samuel 16:13) when 'Samuel took the horn of oil, and anointed him in the midst of his brethren: and the Spirit of the Lord came upon David from that day forward.' His father Jesse kept sheep in Bethlehem, and a boy David had tended the family flock, which, symbolically enough, marks him as both king and shepherd (I Samuel 16:11; II Samuel 7:8). Numbered among David's children by Bathsheba, the former wife of Uriah (II Samuel 12:24; 11:27) are both Solomon and Nathan (I Chronicles 3:5), which makes them blood brothers together with Shamua and Shobab, and a similar statement occurs at II Samuel 5:14.

The two nativity stories clearly differentiate between the Jesus of Matthew, who traces the descendants of Solomon of the kingly line, and the Jesus of Luke, whose concern is Nathan of the priestly line. Solomon figures large in Hebrew history, but very little seems to be known about his brother Nathan. Indeed, the only reference to Nathan is in the list of David's children referred to in the previous paragraph—the same individual who is listed in Luke's genealogy (3:31). There is, however, much mention of Nathan the prophet, he who castigated David about his shameful scheme for procuring Bathsheba for wife. What is certain is that Solomon gave rise to one line of descent ending with the Jesus mentioned in Matthew, and that Nathan gave rise likewise to the Jesus of Luke.

It is well known that two Messiahs were expected, and the prophet Balaam is often quoted in support of this contention. It was said of him that 'he knew the knowledge of the most High', saw 'the vision of the Almighty', and proclaimed, 'I shall see him, but not now: I shall behold him, but not nigh: there shall come a Star out of Jacob, and a sceptre shall rise out of Israel...' (Numbers 24:16–17) This passage seems clearly to be anticipating respectively two separate characters, one priestly and the other kingly, and these are representative of the two Jesuses mentioned in Luke (Nathan the priest) and Matthew (Solomon the king) respectively. The early Christian document The Testaments of the Twelve Patriarchs mentions that 'A lord out of Levi shall awake a high priest, and out of Judah a king, God and man.' The chronicler Flavius Josephus reported that the Essenes were also expecting the appearance—presumably at the same time—of two Messiahs.

The Essene community's Manual of Discipline stated that 'in the last days' (which soon followed, as marked by the destruction of Jerusalem in AD 70), a priestly and a Davidic Messiah were expected to appear, and that 'there shall come a prophet (in the person of John the Baptist) and the Messiah of Aaron (priestly) and Israel' (kingly). Similar passages appear in the so-called Damascus Document.

It is clear from the genealogical tables that both Matthew and Luke include David, the first King of Israel, as ancestor. The line is of *descent* in Matthew, from the past to the present, commencing with the patriarch Abraham through to David, and ending with one 'born Jesus, who is called Christ'. Abraham was instrumental as 'father of the chosen people' in sealing the old covenant with Yahweh, and is the key figure in the establishment of the new, 42 generations on. Luke's Gospel traces the ancestry in line of *ascent*, from Jesus through David to Abraham and beyond—right up to God himself, from the present to the past. By so doing he establishes a 'divine' pedigree as well as a human one. In neither account is the name of the mother mentioned. It is noteworthy that the two genealogies coincide name by name from David to Abraham only. Luke lists 77 names in contrast to

Matthew's 42, a matter that will closely concern us later. It is worth positing that the Luke Jesus was settled on by orthodoxy to be *the* Jesus because of the greater attention Luke paid to the lavishly various details attaching to his nativity story, which contrasts sharply with the much less detailed Matthew account, despite the fact that his Jesus was born into royalty, which status led to the infamous massacre of the infants by Herod.

The purpose of the inclusion of the nativity stories in Matthew and Luke is often a matter for conjecture among biblical scholars, and for them the problem remains. In face of formidable difficulties, some theologians and scholars quail, and understandably so, as uncertainties of translation and perplexities of interpretation abound, not to mention the tracing of intricacies involving citations and typologies in the Old Testament Scriptures, which bristle with overt and covert references, inferences and even wordplay. However, Rudolf Steiner came up with perfectly feasible answers, giving equally convincing reasons for his findings from his investigations into the Akashic Records and other research work.

The biblical Scriptures, both Old and New Testaments, give more than ample indications of the enormous importance of the coming event of a sojourn on earth, albeit necessarily brief—only three years or so—of an exalted hierarchical Being, one so lofty as to be designated as the Son of God himself. Upon reflection, it seems absurd to imagine that such a Being should be born to a seemingly ordinary couple, or at least regarded as not so very extraordinary, in a cowshed manger. It seems somewhat remarkable that orthodox Christian teachings should dwell on minor details, as the fact that the father of Jesus was a mere carpenter, though the mother was chosen to be so exceptionally glorified, so excessively exalted, as to become an object of worship. What is still more remarkable is that the glaring discrepancies between the two lists of ancestors, those of Matthew and Luke, are so commonly disregarded and given so little importance as to be dismissed as details not warranting serious attention.

As Rudolf Steiner has convincingly shown, such an event is not only of earthly importance but one of cosmic significance also, as indicated repeatedly throughout this book. What he presents is not so much rooted in belief but rather in fact. Indeed, his message is one with a truly scientific basis, and does not depend on mere trust or faith alone. The customary failing that weakens all kinds of belief is that it can—and all too often does—give rise to opinion and argument, which leads on unfailingly to divisive sectarianism. There can be few genuine counter-arguments to his supersensory investigations and findings because of their sound qualities of coherence and truth, and hence—eventually if persevered with—they will be accepted as valid. The main reason why his work is so slowly being recognized is that its language is unfamiliar, and the notions he posits are very innovative. Undoubtedly, the study of spiritual science requires an open mind as well as patience and perseverance, but gradually its really convincing quality, which rests on its genuinely scientific nature and structure, leads to trust—and eventually in many instances to personal experience.

The two nativity stories

Written by a Jew with Jewish Christians in mind, Matthew's Gospel, not unnaturally, emphasized the notion of Jesus as King of the Jews, thereby fostering the Messianic hopes and expectations of the people. The Magi were seeking 'he that is born King of the Jews' (Matthew 2:2), and the chief priests and scribes undoubtedly knew all about the Old Testament prophecies concerning this extraordinarily important event. This is almost to be expected, as Bethlehem in Judaea, some six miles south of Jerusalem, was regarded as the City of David and the ancestral line of the Matthew Jesus was traceable back to David through Solomon, who succeeded David as King of Israel. The royal line of descent from David through Solomon is nicely reflected in Matthew's account of the nativity, whereas Luke's account, in which the ancestry is traced back to David via Nathan, reflects the pastoral and priestly line.

Rudolf Steiner confirmed that the Essenes were well aware of this 42-generation path to a situation whereby individuals who had undertaken it were then free of all hereditary influences. Having reached this degree of purity, or even divinity, and been admitted to the earthly Mysteries, they were regarded as qualified candidates for admission to the higher cosmic Mysteries. Obversely, divine entities who sought to descend to the earth would likewise take 42 generations, and this is evidenced by Matthew's genealogy figuring these in the case of the Christ Being. His ancestral register shows Jesus at 41 and Christ at 42, thus indicating his true status—at the end, be it noted. Thus, whatever else has been said of this arrangement, it vouchsafes the divinity of the Christ Being.

In the case of Luke's list of 77, the Divine Father is placed first, at the beginning. This is a further example of the pattern of poise and counterpoise or reversal, which can be detected elsewhere, e.g. the one becoming two and the two becoming one in the case of Adam and Eve, the Matthew and Luke

Jesuses becoming one, and the Holy Spirit and Jesus of Nazareth blending to form Christ Jesus, all in true archetypal fashion. Matters involving heredity must involve both physical and etheric principles of the infant Jesus of Matthew's Gospel, as one who could cope with the powers and capabilities possessed by Zarathustra. In the Gospel of Luke, this genealogy of Jesus is presented in line of *descent* and by this very token it is indicated that the child had a divine origin; this is further indicated by tracing the lineage via Adam right back to God himself. By the same token, the powers and capabilities attaching to the Nirmanakaya of the Buddha was bestowed on the Luke Jesus, as will be further discussed in Chapter 5.

Firm details are always difficult to ascertain, and the odd—sometimes very odd—snippets from the apocryphal writings add a little colour to these stories, as well as a smile or two. For example, the apocryphal Book of James reports Joseph to be an old man, and a widower. When required to go to the temple for the choosing of a future husband for Mary he protested on the grounds of his age, saying that he had sons of his own, and that he would be ridiculed when seen to be married to such a young girl. Notwithstanding this, he was chosen from among several other candidates to become the husband of Mary, who according to some traditions was 16 years old at the time. The History of Joseph the Carpenter, also an apocryphal book, states that Joseph was 40 years of age when he married, and that he lived with Mary for two years before she gave birth to Jesus—but it must have been the Luke Mary, whose husband was by tradition a carpenter.

In Luke's account the angelic annunciation to Mary was when she was in the sixth month of her pregnancy and living in Nazareth, some 60 miles north of Jerusalem in Galilee. The evangelist takes care to mention that she was espoused to Joseph, of the house of David (Luke 1:26–7). It was necessary for Joseph and Mary to make this long journey of some 66 miles to Bethlehem in order to be taxed (Luke 2:4,5). After the birth and circumcision of their baby Jesus in Bethlehem, and on their way back home 'to their own city of Nazareth', they called in at the temple in Jerusalem in order to present, or 'devote', him in customary fashion to the Lord (2:22, 39). Thereafter, the family returned to their home town of Nazareth (Luke 2:39). Throughout his Gospel there is no mention of any other offspring, so it is certain that the Luke Jesus was an only child.

It is significant that Luke does not introduce his genealogical table until *after* the baptism of Jesus—by now an adult, of course—by John the Baptist in the River Jordan. Matthew places his account of this event in a more likely spot, namely, at the start of Chapter 1, immediately before his nativity story. Both Abraham and David were key figures in the history of the Hebrews, and it is also significant that the inconsistencies in agreement of the genealogies of Matthew and Luke appear at David, the first King of Israel. Abraham, 'the man who has seen God', was the prototype of the people of Israel. He was especially chosen by God, who made a covenant with him, indicating the very special relationship with Abraham and his descendants. It is noteworthy that there were two lines of descent from Abraham, those of Isaac and Ishmael, and two from David 14 generations later, namely, Solomon and Nathan. Both Ishmael and Solomon were thus partly of foreign blood—the Egyptian Hagar in the case of Ishmael and presumably Hittite in the case of Bathsheba, as Uriah was of that people. This election of Abraham, according to Paul (Gal. 3:7, 29), extends the terms of the covenant, so that everyone 'who is Christ's' is considered to be 'issue' of Abraham, thus pointing up the universal character of Christianity in terms of salvation. The 'old' covenant or testament is thus renewed by the 'new' testament which is inherent in the life and works of Christ Jesus. By authority of the genealogies Jesus is firmly established as belonging to the family and lineage of David; there is no doubt as to his royal pedigree.

Now David was a shepherd as well as a king, and as if by cue it is shepherds of the field who attend the baby Jesus in Luke's Gospel, appropriately enough in a stable in the company of the traditional ox and ass (Isaiah 1:3), whereas the Three 'Kings' or Magi duly attended the Jesus who descended from King Solomon in a house (Matthew 2:11). Matthew wished to leave no doubt in the reader's mind that the Jesus whose birth he described was of royal descent, as he refers to this fact no fewer that eight times in his Gospel. Symbolically enough, the 'pastoral staff' or crozier, which is carried before or by bishops and other church dignitaries as symbols of their office in modern times, is reminiscent of the shepherd's crook. There are also numerous references to shepherds, lambs and sheep found in both the Old and New Testaments, as in Psalm 23, Isaiah 53:7 and John 1:29; 21:15–16. Significantly, during those times the sun, in its retrogressive path around the earth, was transiting the sign of Aries or the Ram.

Isaiah (60:6) echoes as proof-text Psalm 72:10 in foretelling the visit of the Magi: '... all dromedaries of Midian and Epha; all they from Sheba shall come: they shall bring gold and incense; and they shall show forth the praises of the Lord.' It might seem strange that in Matthew's account Herod—or anyone else for that matter—is not mentioned as seeing the guiding star that indicated the place where the baby

Jesus could be found (Matthew 2:8–9). It is stated that the Wise Men saw it, but it is not reported that anyone else did. It is logical to conjecture that Herod himself could also have followed the star, as being the obvious thing to do, but there is no mention by Matthew of such a happening. The most likely reason was that the star was perceivable only by the Magi, who were taking advantage of their clairvoyant powers to detect the presence of Zarathustra or Zoroaster, the 'Golden Star' who was to provide the Matthew Jesus child with his own etheric body, as will be discussed on pp. 122–6.

The Matthew family lived in a house in Bethlehem itself, in which Jesus was born (Matthew 2:8–11), a considerably more dignified environment than a cow byre or cave, as described in Luke's Gospel. The visitation by the Magi was to a child born into more fitting surroundings, and whose ancestors included Solomon, the son chosen by David, himself king first of Judah and subsequently of all Israel, to succeed him on the throne. In the apocryphal Armenian Gospel of the Infancy, Book XI, the 'Wise Men' or Magi are reported to be kings in their own right: Melkon (of Persia), Gaspar (of India), and Balthasar (of Arabia). As might be expected, they brought rich and rare gifts as befitted a child of royal descent, who was feared by Herod and regarded by the occupying Roman authorities as King of the Jews (Matthew 27:11). Herod, determined that neither he nor his descendants should be threatened by a rival king in the shape of Matthew's baby Jesus, ordered the infamous 'massacre of the innocents' (2:13–17).

Not only Herod was 'troubled' about all this but so too were the people of Jerusalem (Matthew 3:3); and this contrasts strongly with the wonder and enthusiasm of the simple, unsophisticated shepherds reported by Luke (2:10), to whom an angel brought 'good tidings of great joy'. Moreover, the secular, 'earthly' concerns of Herod contrast sharply with the spiritual, 'heavenly' matters brought to the notice of the shepherds. The worldly interests of Herod, jealous of his throne and prepared to employ violence to preserve it, differ strikingly from the gentle, pious goings-on in the temple involving Simeon and Anna. There is an unmistakable emphasis in Matthew on the masculine element. According to Matthew an angel visits Joseph on three occasions, all of them in dreams (1:20; 2:13; 2:19), whereas in Luke, the angel Gabriel's appearance was to Mary (1:26–8). Herod and the Magi are male, whereas Luke's account is dominated by women, as indicated by the friendship of Elisabeth and Mary, and the visitations to Mary by the angel Gabriel. Matthew's account lays stress on the outer concerns, whereas in Luke there is a definite quality of inwardness and piety.

Thus the two families found themselves living in what is reported to have been the small settlement of Nazareth, and it could be expected that they became well acquainted with one another. Steiner asserted from his own investigations that the two families, and hence the two boys, were close friends. It was when both Jesuses were twelve, or at least at a time soon after the incident in the temple reported by Luke (2:41–52), that the Matthew Jesus died. Soon after this the Luke Mary died, as also did the Matthew Joseph; and so it was that a new family was set up, comprising the Luke Joseph and the Matthew Mary, and their son Jesus.

Neither Jesus nor John the Baptist, who according to Luke (1:36) was about six months older than he, were among the children massacred. The Matthew Jesus was safe in Egypt (2:13), being taken there by his parents to the comparative safety of Nazareth only after the death of Herod (2:23).

Tradition has it that the Matthew Jesus was about two months old when the flight into Egypt was made, where the family are said to have remained for four years. Oddly enough, there is no mention of any massacre in Luke, despite the likelihood that such an unforgettably monstrous atrocity would remain long in the public memory. One can only conjecture, given the premise that the accounts in Matthew and Luke are *both* true, that the Luke Jesus as well as John the Baptist were born at about the same time (Luke 1:24, 63) after the massacre had taken place. Matthew is very vague as to the time of the nativity he describes, merely stating that it took place 'in the days of King Herod' (1:1), whereas Luke reports his birth story as happening in the time when Caesar Augustus was Emperor of Rome (30 BC to AD 14), also when Herod was in power. Clearly, such details are insufficient to be of any help in clarifying such matters, which are not of such great importance anyway.

Matthew's Joseph, having been warned by an angel in a dream, escaped with Mary and baby Jesus into Egypt (Matthew 2:13–14), there to remain for a few years (three according to the apocryphal Arabic Gospel of the Infancy). Upon their return, Joseph was warned, again in a dream, not to go to Bethlehem, but to 'turn aside into parts of Galilee', and accordingly the family 'went and dwelt in a city called Nazareth' (Matthew 2:22–3), the home town of the Luke family. The Matthew family became quite sizeable in the course of time, for after Jesus, who was the firstborn son (Matthew 1:23), were born James, Joses, Judas and Simon (Matthew 13:55; 27:56; Mark 6:3; 15:40, 47;16:1), as well as two sisters, commonly understood to be Salome and (perhaps) Mary (Mark 15:40).

The actuality, then, was that the Luke Joseph and Mary

had one son only, and it was he who eventually grew up as Jesus of Nazareth, for this couple's home was in Nazareth (Luke 1:26; 2:39). He was their only child, named by Mary on the instructions of the angel at the Annunciation. Similarly, the firstborn of the Matthew Joseph and Mary was also named Jesus—but by his father (Matthew 1:25), who was instructed in a dream to name the expected son Jesus (1:21). This couple was domiciled in Bethlehem (2:1). Both mothers are reported to be virginal (Matthew 1:25, Luke 2:7). After their flight to Egypt the Matthew couple did not return to Bethlehem, but on instructions, not surprisingly given to Joseph in a dream, they made their way to Nazareth to dwell there, thus fulfilling the prophesy that this would occur (Matthew 2:23).

Important numbers and their significance

The fundamental constitution of the human being comprises body, soul and spirit, and it was necessary for the provision of these principles from sources that had been brought to the highest possible state of perfection. It was imperative that such an impeccably ideal vehicle for occupancy by such an exalted spiritual being as the Christ could scarcely be provided from a single source, and this was indeed the case. According to Rudolf Steiner, the perfected physical body was contributed by the Hebrew people in 42 generations; its sustaining accessory in the form of its flawless, wisdom-filled etheric body was supplied by Zarathustra, and its sublimely consummate astral body was supplied by the exalted and accomplished Buddha.

The general concept of human nature as dual in constitution, as body and soul, is replaced nowadays by the assumption of the human being as threefold, namely, body, mind (rather than soul) and spirit. However, a fourfold pattern arises by dint of the biblical notion of the reality of human beings comprising body, soul and spirit, in which resides the 'I Am', the ego which is experienced by all human beings and vouchsafed to Moses by God himself as a divine gift, as his 'memorial unto all generations' (Exodus 3:15). Our physical-material body maintains its life by means of its supportive etheric body, and these taken together are often referred to as our 'corporeal' nature. This in turn is indwelt by our 'soul-spiritual' nature, a term that is self-evident. Thus the model is seen to revert to being a dual one. Steiner averred that these two sets of natures, obviously differing in terms of function and attributes, necessitated the highest possible degree of perfection required by the exalted Being known as the Christ during the time he was to abide on the earth. It therefore ensued that the corporeal members were to be supplied by the Matthew Jesus and the soul-spiritual members by the Luke Jesus. This arrangement was necessary because the Jesus who was later to be known as Jesus of Nazareth was required to be totally undefiled in order to be a fitting human being for the Christ Being to incarnate into.

Distinct patterns of threefolding and sevenfolding are also evident in the 42 ancestors listed by Matthew and the 77 by Luke, for which orthodox theology sees fit for the most part to ignore. The three seven-year maturational stages in human beings of infancy, childhood and adolescence mark the development of the physical (0–7), etheric (7–14) and astral (14–21) principles. Rudolf Steiner contended that this pattern can be seen to operate in archetypal fashion at the evolutionary level also, in that succeeding generations also progress in similar fashion. He further contended that an individual's genetic characteristics do not manifest in children of the next generation, but in that of their grandparents, that is to say, every other generation, which renders the number 14 even more important.

Matthew (1:20) is careful to remind readers that Joseph was the son of David, thus echoing the messianic prophecy made to David. Only in Luke are the 21 (3 × 7) generations from Abraham to God recorded. From Abraham to David the 14 generations are mentioned in both Matthew and Luke, agreeing in name and order. From David through Solomon to Jesus in Matthew (the kingly line) are 28 generations, 14 to the time when Jeconiah and his retinue were made to go to Babylon, and a further 14 to Jesus the Christ. The 42nd step is represented by that from Jesus to Christ at his baptism by John in the River Jordan.

The 3 × 14 pattern (or 6 × 7) in Matthew is significant from several points of view. Seven sevens are 49, important in Judaism as a jubilee year, making a fresh start with the 50th, which was always regarded as a rest year when land was left fallow and all debts forgiven. As Rudolf Steiner pointed out, this marked the beginning of a Cosmic New Year. Now it was imperative that Jesus of Nazareth, who was destined to receive the Christ Being at the baptism by John in the River Jordan, was to be immaculate in every sense of the word. The three essentially human members, physical, etheric and astral, which had all reached the stage of perfection, had been carefully prepared during the preceding 42 (3 × 14) generations registered by Matthew. Thus was prepared the Jesus who at his birth had received such a mightily advanced individuality as Zarathustra. It was he who taught that the sun was not only the supreme life-giver to the earth by means of its light and warmth, but also the dwelling-place of Ormuzd or Ahura Mazda, the Creator of the world and the source of all wisdom.

With regard to these facts the Roman Catholic scholar S.J. Binz, in his book *The Advent of the Savior,* makes some interesting observations from a rather different point of view:

The 3 times 14 pattern in Matthew is interestingly deliberate. There were 14 days from the new moon to the full moon, the beginning of the Jewish month, to the full moon, the day of Israel's greatest feasts, Passover and Tabernacles. Thus, both David and Jesus are preceded by 14 waxing generations, beginning with the new moon of Abraham and the darkness of the Exile. The full luminance represents the reign of David and the advent of Christ. It is also significant that the letters for David in Hebrew (d-w-d) have the numerical value of 14 $(4+6+4)$. Thus the pattern of the generations expresses the fact that Jesus is indeed the Messiah, the long-awaited Son of David. Considering this division of history, Jesus was preceded by six periods of generations (3×14). The reign of the Messiah opened the seventh period of seven, the period of fullness and completion. The advent of Christ marked the end of God's careful plan.

Rudolf Steiner, in his lecture given in Bochum on 21 December 1913 (not translated into English) had this to say:

The Nathan (Luke) Jesus was absolutely pure. His soul had been preserved or held back by the higher Hierarchies, and was untainted by luciferic temptation and influences. Thus he had rescued love in its highest manifestation—totally innocent. Therefore, he had no life experience that could have been won from many incarnations. But this was done at a stroke by the passing over of the Solomon (Matthew) Jesus soul, which was that of Zarathustra, as 'bearer of the supreme achievements of human culture'. The Luke Jesus received the astral body of the Buddha as being as it were the purest available.

Some further notions

There was much discussion among the early Church worthies concerning the brothers and sisters of Jesus. Helvidius thought they made up a single family, and Jerome that they were merely cousins. Epiphanius held that they were children of Joseph by a previous wife. The much-used term 'son of Mary' in the Gospels, notably Mark and John, also gives much food for contention. Many thought that it indicated that Joseph was now dead (as he probably was by then), as it was not customary for contemporary Jews to refer to a man by the name of his mother.

Bearing in mind the proposition that it was the Matthew Mary's son who died after the event of the two Jesuses becoming one, it must have been the Luke Jesus who survived. It was this Jesus who was born and bred in Nazareth, and he it was who was taken by his parents to Jerusalem, and was the boy who declared that he must be about *his Father's* business. Now he was obviously not referring to his natural father; and it must be emphasized that it is Luke who traces the ancestry of Jesus back to God himself—his 'spiritual' Father (Luke 3:38). This also infers that it was the Matthew Jesus who died; in other words, the boy who survived the uniting of the two was clearly the Luke Jesus. Moreover, it is significant that the account of the incident in the temple appears only in Luke's Gospel.

How, then, did the one surviving child, the only child, of the Luke Mary come to be counted in and accepted as a member of the sizeable family of the Matthew Mary? As has been contended, the Matthew Joseph and the Luke Mary both died before the baptism of Jesus in the River Jordan, and both families were known to have resided in Nazareth. This is an intriguing problem, and the most feasible solution would lie in the contention that the widowed Matthew Mary and the Luke Joseph, a widower, united as one family, and this, according to Steiner, was what happened. Such an arrangement would explain why the Luke Jesus, himself an only child, appears in the accounts of both Matthew and Mark as part of a sizeable family. Notable in view of this explanation is the entire absence in the account by Luke of the mention of any family, or what this should be.

John's Gospel does not include a nativity story, and it is probable that even by the time that he wrote it (*c*. AD 85), there was no tradition of virginal conception. He mentions Joseph on two occasions (John 1:45; 6:42), both referring simply to 'Jesus, son of Joseph'. Mark mentions Mary as the mother of Jesus only once, but does not name the two sisters (Mark 6:3). It may be significant that there is no occasion that John actually mentions Mary by name, but cites her as 'the mother of Jesus'. The story of the marriage in Cana (2:1, 3), makes no mention of Joseph or indeed of any father. She— again not mentioned by name—is reported to have been present at the crucifixion. 'Mary the mother of Jesus, and with his brethren' are mentioned in Acts 1:14, and in this connection it is interesting to recall that Luke was the writer of Acts. As Jesus is mentioned together with 'his brethren' it is reasonable to contend that this mother of Jesus was the Matthew Mary.

All this supports Steiner's statement that the Luke Joseph had died by then, the Matthew Joseph having died much earlier. That we do not know what details were left out renders it very difficult to pull the loose ends of the Gospel accounts together. Rudolf Steiner attested from his investigations that Jesus of Nazareth was about 24 years of age when his father (the Luke Joseph) died, and that from that time onwards he maintained close connections with the Essenes and their teachings; he did not actually become a member of their community however. At that time, asserted Steiner, there were four thousand members. By rigorously following certain rules, which were recorded in the various documents of the Dead Sea Scrolls, they were able to raise themselves to the stage when they were capable of supersensory perception into the spiritual worlds. This capability was, needless to say, already possessed by Jesus.

After his baptism in the River Jordan, Jesus went to his home town of Nazareth in order to preach in the synagogue there. The local people were astounded, and said: 'Is not this Joseph's son?' (Luke 4:22). Similarly, Matthew (13:54–6), Mark (6:1–3) and (John 6:42) report precisely the same event, when the astonished populace asked: 'Is not this the carpenter's son? Is not his mother Mary?' as if to implicate that Joseph (of the Matthew nativity account) had died by then, and this would be feasible if, as by apocryphal tradition, he was already past middle age when he fathered Jesus. Again, Steiner confirms that this was indeed the case.

On this occasion Jesus is vexed with the citizens of Nazareth *and his mother* because of their 'unbelief'. Even his own family did not acknowledge his new role as Messiah, for these events took place soon after his baptism in the River Jordan. The local people recognize him as the carpenter's son, asking where and how a former mere tradesman had suddenly acquired this new wisdom and power. (Here the reference to 'the carpenter's son' identifies him as the Luke Jesus.) Oddly enough, however, Mary and his brothers and sisters seemed not to acknowledge him as the Messiah. The fact that they recognized him as one of the family, but do not, in a certain sense, want to know him, tells its own story.

The whole problem of the two Jesuses outlined in this chapter though reasonably explicable is rather brief, but there can be no substitute for reading the numerous lecture courses given by Rudolf Steiner for oneself. This includes his course of lectures which he called *The Fifth Gospel*, and *Christianity as Mystical Fact*, a written work based on lectures he gave in 1902.

The scholar Robert Reisenman, in his book *James, the Brother of Jesus*, mentions the received teaching since the end of the fourth century that James was the brother of Jesus of Nazareth, not only by a different father, an obvious fact in view of the divine sonship, but also by a *different mother*. The answer to this conundrum, he contends, is regarded to have been solved by devising the notion of the perpetual virginity of Mary. Naturally, these notions are orthodox, being constructed on the premise that there was only one Mary and only one Joseph. Whatever else, the actuality was, according to Rudolf Steiner, that the Luke Jesus was stepbrother to the Matthew Mary's six children. At Luke 3:23 we read: 'And Jesus himself began to be about thirty years of age, being (*as was supposed*), the son of Joseph, which was the son of Heli ...' etc. Heli was named by Luke as the father of Joseph, thus neatly identifying him as Jesus of Nazareth's grandfather (Luke 3:23). At 13:55–6, Matthew has the people of Nazareth saying: 'Is this not the carpenter's son? Is not his mother called Mary? And his brethren, James, and Joses, and Simon, and Judas? And his sisters, are they not all with us? Whence then hath this [*man*] all these things?'

By way of explanation, Steiner asserted that soon after the incident in the temple, the Luke Mary died. In the course of events the Matthew Joseph also died, and the Luke Joseph married or otherwise cohabited with the Matthew Mary as a family. The 'composite' Jesus (of Nazareth) therefore assumed the role-relationship of stepbrother to these six children. Thus, typically true to the pattern of destiny, the two families also thus became one. This account of events supplies a tidy answer to Eisenman's problem.

There are other pointers in this direction to be found in Mark's Gospel. At Mark 6:3 Jesus is referred to as the 'son of Mary', whereas by custom his father, had he been alive, would have been mentioned rather than the mother. This upholds Steiner's assertion that the Luke Joseph died late in the 18-year period between the temple incident and Jesus' baptism by John in the River Jordan. Mark's parallel account is of the former Jesus of Nazareth's first visit to 'his own country' together with his disciples and hordes of followers after his baptism by John in the River Jordan. The personality changes were such that his old acquaintances were 'astonished' at his newly acquired 'wisdom' evidenced by his teachings in the synagogue, and were 'offended' by his 'mighty works'. He appeared to be a very different person to the lad who had left home some years before to go on his travels which, according to Steiner, included visiting the Essene community. He now had his own disciples, could cast out devils, and was being followed everywhere by great multitudes of people. His old friends and family imputed that he was actually 'beside himself' (Mark 3:21), and in this they were in fact not far wrong. He had left them as Jesus of Nazareth, but returned as Jesus the Christ.

Strangely—but not so strangely, perhaps—Luke does not mention such goings-on. He made it plain by relating the temple event, ensuring that the lineage of Jesus of Nazareth be traceable through David to God himself. The contents of the first three chapters are loaded with fulfilments of prophecies and other preparatory material, and the connections with John the Baptist are made plain. There are no surprises. The temptations trial (Matthew 4:1–11; Luke 4:1–13) having been successfully overcome, the former Jesus of Nazareth, but now Christ Jesus, made bold enough on his first visit as such to the synagogue in 'his own country' to 'preach the acceptable year of the Lord', proclaiming a world jubilee year (Luke 4:16–19).

The incident in the temple

Further matters of interest include the well-known incident in the temple in Jerusalem during the annual feast of the Passover. An account of this incident appears only in Luke, (2:42–52) and it repays close study. Significantly after three days, the Luke parents were upset and confused when they returned to the temple to find their son Jesus a very different boy in character but not in looks. When Mary and Joseph, having 'lost' Jesus in the crowds, returned to Jerusalem they found their son Jesus in the temple, 'sitting in the midst of the doctors, both hearing them and asking them questions, and all that heard him were astonished at his understanding and answers' (Luke 2:46–7). They were amazed at this, and it was 'his mother' who said to the boy, addressing Jesus as 'Son' (Authorized Version), 'My Son' (New English Bible), that she and his 'father' had sought him sorrowing. Strangely enough, Luke has Mary, 'his mother', addressing Jesus as *teknon* (child) rather than *huios* (son) as might be expected, thus revealing more than a hint of confusion. Without doubt he was her son, but it would seem in outward appearance only. (This is a typical example of 'rationalized translation', but it is feasible in that the boy Jesus's real mother could not entirely believe that this genius of a boy could possibly be hers, hence the use of the world 'child' rather than the more likely 'son'. The translators could not take her at her word!)

Everyone, including the boy's parents, were astounded at his newly acquired depth of erudition and wisdom in both sacred and secular affairs. Hitherto she had known her son as loving, gentle and guileless, of innocent demeanour and purity of character. Moreover, this incident is reported only by Luke, and this confirms that the 'child' was indeed their own son. As already pointed out, Luke is careful to introduce a 'heavenly' father also—significantly *after* reporting the baptism in the Jordan, for he reveals this in his genealogy in the previous chapter by tracing the boy's ancestry right back to God himself (Luke 2:48). Jesus's 'earthly' father's business was that of a carpenter, as noted by Matthew (13:55) and Mark (6:3), though not by Luke.

So, within the space of two chapters we have Joseph, the earthly father of Jesus (of Nazareth) and God as heavenly 'Father'; and here Luke is pointing to the certain destiny of the twelve-year-old Luke Jesus as providing the physical vehicle for the Christ. The significance of Luke's putting his genealogy at Chapter 3 (verse 38) and not at the 'natural' place for it, namely, at the start of his Gospel as Matthew does, has already been indicated. Rudolf Steiner confirmed that it was around this time, namely, when the two Jesus boys were about twelve years old, at about the time of the temple incident, that the Matthew Joseph and the Luke Mary died, and the families combined, living as they both were in Nazareth. Mary did not understand Jesus' words, but the passage 'But his mother kept all these sayings in her heart' (Luke 2:51) may well refer to some kind of further revelation to this Mary connected with the message of the shepherds twelve years earlier (Luke 2:19) which she also 'pondered in her heart'.

There is no account of any such event in Matthew's Gospel. It may or may not be significant but is nonetheless interesting that he employs the word *paidiou* (little child) throughout Chapter 2 (8, 9, 11, 13 twice, and at 14, 20 and 21). It is only at 2:15 that he employs 'my son' (*ton huion mou*), but this is in connection with the prophecy by 'the Lord' that he should be called out of Egypt, and not in course of the narrative.

Some entertaining signals

The bare facts of the genealogies point to the certainty that there were indeed two boys called Jesus, both of whose parents were called Joseph and Mary. Another fact is that there was only one Jesus of Nazareth, so the question arises: which of these two boys survived and grew to manhood? It is interesting, and sometimes entertaining, to survey the apocryphal gospels and scriptures, and the world of art, for supporting indications that there were indeed two boys and not only one, as common sense would suggest in spite of the conflicting birth stories. In the Pistis-Sophia (meaning Faith-Wisdom), a Gnostic gospel text dating from the second century, which was regarded as heretical by the young Church, the following quaint passage appears:

Mary answered and said: ... Thy Power prophesied through David: Grace (*charis*) and Truth (*aletheia*) are met together, Righteousness and Peace have kissed each other. Truth hath flourished out of the earth, and Righteousness hath looked down from heaven. Thus did thy Power prophesy once concerning thee. When thou wast little, before the Spirit came upon thee, the Spirit came from the height whilst thou wast in a vineyard with Joseph, and came unto mine house in thy likeness, and I knew it not, and I thought that it was thou. And the Spirit said to me: Where is Jesus my brother, that I may meet with him? And when it spake thus to me, I was in perplexity, and thought that it was a phantom come to tempt me. I took it therefore and bound it to the foot of the bed that was in mine house, until I should go forth unto thee and Joseph in the field and find you in the vineyard, where Joseph was staking the vineyard. It came to pass then, that when thou heardest me tell the matter to Joseph, thou understoodest the matter, and didst rejoice, and say: Where is he, that I may behold him? Otherwise I will tarry for him in this place.

And it came to pass, when Joseph heard these words, he was troubled: and we went together and entered into the house and found the Spirit bound to the bed. And we looked upon thee and upon it, and found that thou wert like to him; and he that was bound to the bed was loosed, and embraced thee and kissed thee, and thou kissedst him, and ye became one.

(Taken from the Theosophical Publishing Society edition, 1896)

Here, it is clear that Mary is making reference to Psalm 85:10,11: 'Mercy and truth are met together; righteousness and peace have kissed each other. Truth shall spring out of the earth; and righteousness shall look down from heaven.' Christ was often referred to as the 'Sun of Righteousness', as in Malachi 4:2, or the 'Prince of Peace', as in Isaiah 9:6, and is mentioned in John 1:14, 17 as being 'full of grace and truth', and as furnishing the channel for these attributes (1:17).

Mary seems to be speaking to Jesus about what happened when he was still a boy, before he was baptized, when 'the Spirit came upon' him. This Spirit is described as coming from 'the height', which is indicative of heaven or the spiritual worlds; and the confused state in which Mary reported herself to be is readily understandable. There is confirmation that the two boys knew one other, hence the enthusiastic greeting. The statement, bald and unequivocal as it is, that the two became one, is further indication that this did indeed come about.

Interesting with regard to this account taken from the Gnostic text is a wall painting (see p. 136) by the Italian artist Borgognone (*c*. 1450–1523) in the Church of St Ambrogio in Milan, which has to do with the well-known episode described by Luke (2:41–52). As we know, the Luke Mary, Joseph and their son Jesus had gone on their annual visit to Jerusalem to celebrate the feast of the Passover, and they inadvertently left Jesus in Jerusalem. When they went back to find him, he is found in the temple, 'sitting in the midst of the doctors, both hearing them, and asking them questions'.

However, Borgognone depicts two boys, not one, both with haloes framing their similarly cut long, fair, wavy hair, and wearing similar garments of the same hue of light red ochre. One boy is shown sitting on a raised chair against a background of three domed arches in the centre of the group of elderly scholars, with his right hand over his heart and his

'The twelve-year-old Jesus in the temple' by Borgognone

left hand pointing upwards. He is obviously a healthy, sturdy boy, and he is looking sideways and downwards towards his right and towards the other boy, whose back is towards him. This boy is, however, appreciably smaller and thinner than his counterpart, sickly-looking, utterly lacking in vitality, and with his eyes averted backwards. It is almost as if this frail figure is dematerializing on the spot, and his garment, which is of a noticeably paler shade, is ethereal and semi-transparent. He, too, has his right hand over his heart, but his left arm is sloping downwards and away from his body. In his left hand is what appears to be a small fragment of parchment with ragged, uneven edges. Oddly, perhaps, he seems oblivious of the woman who is standing near the doorway with arms open in a gesture of caring concern. Behind her is a male figure, also haloed, who is obviously Joseph. Several of the priestly figures standing and sitting around are looking at this pale, pathetic-looking boy with obvious sympathy, and the whole atmosphere is one of tense and earnest concern.

Such a picture does no more than exhibit artistic licence, but it is nevertheless indicative of a tradition that there were indeed two Jesus boys. Moreover, at about the time of Bergognone in the fifteenth and sixteenth centuries there was a veritable rash of pictures in similar vein, many of which can be found reproduced in *Die Zwei Jesusknaben in der bildenen Kunst*, by Hella Krause-Zimmer. In the same book appears a reproduction in colour of the painting by Raphael known as the *Madonna Terranuova* (see p. 138), which is now in the Bildarchiv Prüssischer Kulturbesitz in Berlin, and depicts the Madonna with three infant boys. The picture is of a composite nature, with artistic licence taken. One boy, immediately identifiable as John the Baptist, is standing on her right; on her left stands a boy of similar age, dressed in gold brocade cloth. The colour and quality of this could indicate that he is of royal descent and is identifiable as the Matthew Jesus. Raphael clearly conveys the notion that it is the Matthew Jesus who is the boy who has no future, as indicated by the fact that Mary's gaze is fixed on the younger Luke Jesus, safe on her lap and who is decidedly the centre of attention. The Matthew Jesus is thus completely ignored by the other two boys, who are also staring at him.

That the child on the Madonna's lap can only be the Luke

'Madonna Terranova' by Raphael

Jesus, the 'priestly' child from the Nathan line, is suggested by a kind of bridge it formed between him and John the Baptist in the shape of a scroll which reads: ECCE AGNIUS DEI, Latin for BEHOLD THE LAMB OF GOD. These are the words used by John the Baptist as recorded by John the Evangelist immediately before (John 1:29), and the day after the baptism in the River Jordan (1:35). It is this boy, the Luke Jesus, who survived to become Jesus of Nazareth whom John the Baptist baptized and who was crucified. All this does not 'prove' anything, but allowing for a little artistic licence, it certainly fits the bill.

A mysterious parallel

Melchizedek is a very mysterious individuality, who is first mentioned in Genesis 14:18 as 'priest of the most high God' who blessed Abraham, granting him knowledge of the Sun Mysteries. He 'brought out bread and wine' for the occasion, thus symbolizing the coming event in the far future of the Last Supper. The implications for the appearance of a future Messiah from Abraham's descendants are clear, as well as those for the future sacramental act of the Eucharist. The erudite writer of the Epistle to the Hebrews was known, according to Origen, only to God, though many scholars think he may well have been Barnabas, the close associate of Paul. In his letter to the Hebrews (5:10; 6:20) he refers to Christ as being a 'high priest for ever after the order of Melchizedek', the proof-text being Psalm 110:4. The whole of the seventh chapter of Hebrews is highly relevant, and it is plain that its writer put very great store indeed on the parallels between Melchizedek and Christ, at the same time hinting that he was not able to go fully into the Mysteries surrounding them (Hebrews 5:8–14), where hints are made that only the initiated could understand the facts of the matter.

In Hebrews 7:1–3, the author states: 'This Melchizedek, king of Salem, priest of God Most High, met Abraham returning from the rout of the kings and blessed him... His name, in the first place, means "king of righteousness"; next he is king of Salem, that is, "king of peace". He has no father, no mother, no lineage, his life no end. He is like the Son of God: he remains a priest for all time.'

Christ Jesus, like Melchizedek, is holy, blameless, undefiled, sinless and 'raised higher than the heavens' (Hebrews

A Greek icon, also depicting a twelve-year-old Jesus in the temple.
(Note second boy to the right of Jesus.)

7:26). Having no sins to expiate, he is in every way perfect, and is therefore eminently suitable for his task of redemption. The inference is clear that Christ, having also been declared Son of God at the baptism in the Jordan, had not been subject to birth and death either, but possessed an existence that is eternal.

5
FIRST ADAM AND SECOND ADAM

The first man is of the earth, earthy; the second man is the Lord from heaven.

I Corinthians 15:47

Matters of authenticity

A significant problem for many people is that of interpreting the Scriptures dealing with the creation of the world and mankind as set out in Genesis. A strictly fundamental approach is not acceptable to most readers, and this is understandable. What such individuals do not fully appreciate, perhaps, is that the narratives were written in ancient times, when the consciousness and ways of thinking were very different from what they are today. Such accounts cannot reasonably be expected to stand up to the rational, intellectualistic habits of modern historical investigators, who recognize and acknowledge them as the legends that they are. This is not to say that they do not possess an authenticity of their own—indeed, they are worthy of the highest respect and regard. It is fortunate that spiritual investigators such as Rudolf Steiner are capable of understanding and interpreting them in the very fashion intended by those ancient chroniclers.

In his lecture cycle *The Effects of Esoteric Development*, for instance, Steiner explains in some detail how such legends of the 'fall' from Paradise and the Holy Grail appear to clairvoyant investigators, and how they may be interpreted. Without this kind of approach it is difficult to arrive at the concept of there being two Adams—the first the Adam of Genesis and the Old Covenant and the second Adam, identifiable as Christ Jesus of the New Covenant as championed by Saul and Paul respectively—without a proper understanding of the two Jesuses mystery. In view of the enormous difficulties in respect of suspending unbelief concerning these matters, perseverance and an open mind are obligatory.

Paul refers to Adam as 'the first man', and to Christ Jesus the 'Son of Man' or 'the Lord out of heaven' as the 'second man', 'the Heavenly One' whom he also refers to as the 'last Adam' (I Corinthians 15:45–9). Robert Reisenman, in his book *James the Brother of Jesus*, points out that 'in turn this means that the knowledge of these doctrines and their identification with the "Christ" comes before the Gospels in their present form . . .' This is so, but the requirement of taking this into practical account by generations of biblical scholars is little short of reprehensible. It was clear to Paul that Adam as the 'first man' is closely associated with the 'second man', the 'Son of Man'. The 'Lord out of heaven' is therefore identifiable as the Christ Being as 'Son of God'. The many contrasts and parallels between the two Adams will now be made clearly discernible.

The first Adam had no parentage except God himself, and was made in his image, and possessed his spiritual nature— and so, by virtue of ancestral lineage, do we all. At his Fall, however, he was obliged to 'descend' into matter, that is to say, he quite literally incarnated—'was made flesh'—as did the second Adam (John 1:14). So the Christ Being, whose mission it was to bring about redemption and salvation for all from their otherwise inevitable fate of degeneration and ultimate extinction, had also to descend into matter. This descent of Adam's progeny is still going on; the further humankind has sunk into matter over the millennia, the more materialistic in outlook has it become. The rate of escalation of the range and capability of the human intellect since the Dark Ages is astounding, but this extension of intellectual brilliance has brought with it a world-view that is almost entirely materialistic. The human race is now reaching its nadir in this respect, hence the cultural deterioration we are presently experiencing. Civilization has indeed reached a crucial period in its evolution.

True to type, just as the first Adam had no parentage, and did not go through the stages of childhood and adolescence, neither did the second Adam. These facts are very supportive of the Adoptionist stance, which has been touched on from time to time throughout. The general understanding is that the Christ Being, as second Adam, was *apparently* the offspring resulting from some kind of liaison between an earthly human Mary and a heavenly Holy Spirit. The passage in Luke 1:35 dealing with the Annunciation demands close (literal) attention: 'The [introduced here] Holy Spirit shall come upon thee, and the power of the Highest shall overshadow thee; therefore also that holy thing which shall be born of thee shall be called the Son of God.' The 'holy thing' referred to is generally believed by some powerful Christian believers to be somehow or other the result of the union of a specially chosen human female and some kind of spiritual being of a high order. This notion, which forms the main substance of the present Chapter, contradicts common sense, but countless numbers of people deem that such an event took place on the grounds that 'with God all things are possible'.

Correlation between the first and second Adams

This proposition is scarcely necessary, as the first Adam was not actually born in the usual sense of the word and, if the parallel is to hold good, the second Adam likewise should not be born either—as mentioned earlier. Christ was never born and, as the pre-existent Logos, can and never will die. This situation obviously provides grist for the Adoptionist mill. The first Adam, utterly spiritual in nature was, together with Eve, expelled from the Garden of Eden as a result of their disobedience. God 'made coats of skins, and clothed them', thus signifying their incarnation into bodies of earthly matter. This is paralleled in the history of the second Adam, who also descended into a 'ready-made' physical-material human body in the form of Jesus of Nazareth. The human body into which he was to descend, however, would have to be as close to perfection as humanly possible, and this body was a 'product' of the two boy Jesuses of impeccable pedigree who combined in order that this be achieved (as explained in Chapter 4). Thus neither the first nor the second Adam was 'born' as commonly understood.

It is abundantly clear, from close scrutiny, that the whole mission of Christ began with his validation as Son of God at his baptism and ended with his resurrection; the two events may therefore be claimed with not quite equal conviction, for it was the first event that inevitably and inexorably led to the last. It necessitated and validated all the events that were to follow; moreover, the whole story concerns Jesus as the Christ, and not only Jesus of Nazareth. This gives yet another certain pointer to the empty claim that Jesus of Nazareth was Jesus the Christ from conception; whether he is the one whose ancestry is traced via Solomon to David by Matthew or whether he is the one traced via Nathan to Solomon by Luke is not identified. These actualities provide further support for the Adoptionist view, which clearly supports the proclamation that the Messiah was the 'Son of God' before the worlds were created (Colossians 1:15), thus sustaining the concept of his being the pre-existent Logos of the first few verses of John's Gospel.

Of the Messiah, the Book of Enoch says that 'from the beginning the Son of Man was hidden, and the Most High preserved him in the presence of his might, and revealed him to the elect.' Paul, it will be remembered, describes Christ before his revelation as 'a mystery, which was kept secret since the world began' (Romans 16:25); and 'when the fullness of time came, God sent forth his son, born of woman' (Galatians: 4:4). According to early tradition, and indeed according to Paul, the Logos had been a 'mystery', kept hidden, and 'shining in darkness' since the time of the Fall, and the time for the heralding of a world jubilee year arrived with the appearance and agency of John the Baptist. Paul, in Colossians 1:26, says that the mystery 'which from the beginning of the world hath been hid in God' (Ephesians 3:9) 'now is made manifest to his saints'. This statement also appears in Romans 16:25 and I Corinthians 2:7, where the Messiah is described as 'the hidden wisdom'. It was not difficult, therefore, for the Messiah or Christ to be equated with the Logos which, in Philo's mind, was identifiable with the 'soul' of the world, for which Christ Jesus said that he had been prepared for since its foundation (Matthew 25:34; John 1:1–2).

Paul, in I Corinthians 15:44–9, makes much of the 'first Adam' or 'man' (*adam* is the Hebrew word for man) and the 'last Adam', stressing that the first was physical and the last spiritual. Those scholars, both ancient and modern, who seek for parallels, typologies, citations, and so on, do not seem to make much if anything of the fact that the first man— Adam—had no lineage, and was indeed originally created to be deathless. His direct 'parent' was God himself, and was originally destined to be, as it were, after the order of Melchizedek, without human parents. But the first Adam, due to his disobedience, became subject to the death of the body, as did all his descendants after him.

In Romans 5:12–19, Paul mentions Adam as being the 'figure' of him who was to come, and points out several parallels, comparisons and contrasts. Again, what does not seem to have occurred to many people is the implication that Adam, the first man, was doomed to die by very dint of his possession of an earthly body, and this predicament also applied to the second Adam. He took the step from the state of the heavenly and spiritual to that of the earthly and bodily; and this is precisely the step that Christ, as the last man, also took. His genealogy was traceable back to Adam and God (Luke 3:38). Just as Adam had no lineage or descendants before becoming subject to death, so Christ, as Logos, also possessed no lineage or family, but had to descend or incarnate into a 'corruptible' fleshly body which had to be provided for him—he was not 'born', just as Adam was not 'born'. As the first man (Adam) helped to bring into being physical vehicles for his successions of descendants, the second man (Christ Jesus) had to rely on one being provided— by none other than one of the descendants of the first man. Just as the first Adam, by dint of the Fall and as a creature of flesh, had as an inevitable consequence to suffer death, so the second Adam, too, had to 'taste death' (Hebrews 2:9). If the human being, as regards his corruptible body, is descended from the first Adam, then by receiving the Being of Christ into his own being such an individual has the possibility of having a second ancestor. This ancestor, however, is he who on the third day after his body had been laid in the earth rose again from the grave.

Rudolf Steiner averred that in the times before the Gospels were written those who were born naturally in the usual way were called 'twice-born', because everyone proceeds from two parents—mother and father. Those who had experienced 'enlightenment' and thus become aware of the spiritual realms were thereby entitled by this token to be called 'once-born' also, as born of the spirit, and therefore 'Children of God'. Conversely, it is therefore acceptable for the Christ Being, as the Word, to 'become flesh' at the baptism of Jesus of Nazareth by John, that is to say, for the once-born (also in the sense of sole) 'only-begotten of the Father, full of (the spiritual qualities) of grace and truth' (John 1:14) to be called 'Son of Man' also. By virtue of this event Paul, at Romans (8:29), was justified in proclaiming that Christ Jesus was fore-ordained to be the *firstborn* of many 'earthly' brethren: 'For whom, he (God) did foreknow, he also did predestinate to be conformed to the image of his Son, that he might be the firstborn among many brethren.' This 'conformation' alludes to the 'incorruptible body' of I Corinthians 15:52–4, which guarantees immortality to these brethren.

The firstborn son of Adam was conceived of his virginal wife, Eve, so what more natural and proper, therefore, than that the second Adam's physical vehicle should also be born of a 'virgin'? Just as the first Adam had no father but God himself, what more right and proper than the provision—in the mind at least—of a divine creative agent in the figure of a 'holy spirit' as 'father' of the second Adam? It is impossible, therefore, to ascribe to the Christ anything in the way of ancestry or genealogy. As 'begotten of the Father', 'God's only Son' and so on, the relationship, so to speak, was a direct one—Spirit proceeding from Spirit. It is therefore not possible even to attempt to argue or postulate that the Christ was in any way 'born' of a fleshly human being. To state that 'Jesus Christ' was born of whichever woman named Mary is therefore to state the impossible.

Strictly speaking, he was not entitled to call himself by the title *ho Christos* until after his baptism in the Jordan, as we have seen. The saying later used by Paul 'Not I, but Christ in me' was realized in Jesus of Nazareth at the time of his baptism, when he became 'Christophorus', the bearer of Christ. Any reference to 'Jesus Christ' by the Evangelists in connection with events before his 'adoption' by God the Father must certainly have been made with the benefit of hindsight.

The Holy Spirit mystery

Broadly speaking, most orthodox Christians can, when contemplating the Trinity and its members, cope somehow with the notion of God the Father and God the Son, but where the Holy Spirit (*hagion pneuma*) is concerned they are not so sure. We are all familiar with the idea of parenthood, family and the close relationships that such terms suggest. Obviously, they are used metaphorically for the most part, but they may be said to possess connotations that are not so very ordinary, as we shall see. The expression Holy Spirit, it might well be contended, seems not to be fully understood even by theologians. The literature dealing with it is for the most part non-committal, scanty and tentative, and a matter of speculation rather than definite notions supported by firm evidence. However, if we go back to basics and read in the Scriptures what is there rather than read into them what is needed to rationalize ambiguous words and seemingly vague expressions, or even resort to eisegesis, we may be able to make good sense of what appears to be bad or dubious syntax.

Most of the faithful have a fair idea of what is meant by *Spirit* within religious contexts, even if they might find it difficult to explain. The main difficulty is the word *Holy* with its many applications. Different English dictionaries stress their particular compilers' own ideas and so make matters worse. The Greek word *hagion* is neuter and refers to things separated and dedicated to the service of God, sacred, worthy of veneration, with implications of purity, blamelessness and suchlike. The mention of the Holy Spirit in connection with the 'virginal conception' poses some interesting aspects. There are definite references to a Trinity at Matthew 28:19 and II Corinthians 13:14 (notably if not suspiciously, both at the very end of their texts).

The concept of the Trinity was not established in the Church until the first Council at Nicaea in 325, and at Constantinople in 381, as a result of the Arian disputes. The Holy Trinity of God as Father, Son and Holy Spirit combined cannot be fully understood if only purely intellectual methods of approaching it be employed. As a single entity with three interrelated and interweaving principles with such indistinct boundaries, it is and probably will continue to remain a mystery to most people. In that it possesses a threefold nature, it manifests a constitution that is clearly archetypal as it can readily be discerned in the whole of nature as well as in ourselves as human beings and in the structuring of our social behaviours in manifold ways.

The question arises in the minds of agnostics and others as to whether we who see God as threefold do so because we ourselves are aware of the application of this principle in countless diverse and multi-faceted ways. We ourselves exhibit much that is indicative of this archetypal rule—or even law—in our very nature, constitution and conduct. Are we copying the Trinity and its works within ourselves, or are we perceiving it as threefold because of all the trichotomies evident in our own make-up and the environment in which we find ourselves?

Another enigmatic area concerns the whole idea of 'sonship', in that if the virginal conception be understood to ascribe parentage to the Holy Spirit we have the bizarre result that the Christ, as the Creative Word, may be considered to have created or at least formed himself. (The *Theotokos* controversy is discussed in Chapter 6.) The Adoptionist stance, on the other hand, is correspondingly strong, because it posits that the Christ is not in any sense 'born', but descends as an already established exalted spiritual entity into the already carefully prepared human body of Jesus of Nazareth. At John 1:14 the usual translation is 'And the Word *became* (*egeneto*) flesh and dwelt (literally 'tabernacled', thus suggestive of a short stay) among us ...' This phrasing clearly does not suggest any birth as usually understood, although the affiliated Greek term (*ginomai*) allows connotations of 'passing out of one state into another, to be changed into'—as was actually the case.

It seems strange, to say the very least, that the Christ Being, if it/he actually was 'the Son of God' from birth (or even conception) was still being doubted as being such when he was 30-odd years of age. The fact is that his contemporaries were so confused as to declare that Christ Jesus was this 'Son' at such a late stage, and not earlier. His pre-existence is firmly established at John 1:1, and most emphatically at 8:58: 'Jesus said unto them, Verily, verily, I say unto you, Before Abraham was, I am.' It was necessary for him to ask, 'Whom say ye that I am?' (Matthew 16:15; Mark 8:29; Luke 9:20). This became convincingly clear only at a very late moment—when he was actually suffering crucifixion, as a Roman soldier came to acknowledge (Mark 15:39): 'And when the centurion, which stood over against him, saw that he had cried out, and gave up the ghost, he said, Truly, this man was the son of God.' There is no doubt that it was indeed 'Jesus of Nazareth, which was crucified; he is risen ...' (Mark 15:6).

The entity that had risen was thus identifiable as the authentic Son of God; the same was he who had been condemned to death by Pontius Pilate, and the same was he who was baptized by John in the River Jordan. This is where the case for Adoptionism becomes forceful to the point of certainty, that is to say, the Christ Being appeared on earth at that moment in time, not 30 years earlier as one of the Jesus boys as a result of 'virginal conception(s)'. Those fundamentalists and others who trace the appearance of Christ on the earth as far back as the birth(s) seem studiously to ignore the carefully recorded list(s) of forebears who were normal mortals. This contention rests on premises which display prejudice of a particularly flagrant nature, not to mention lack of sheer common sense.

Strange, too, is the feeble notion, earnestly cultivated by its supporters, that the event of the baptism had more to do with the introduction of Jesus of Nazareth's mission to the world, to launch a whole body of teachings and perform good deeds of various, often spectacular miracles, healings and so forth. It is significant that the baptismal event marked the end of the

18-year gap between it and the well-known temple episode related by Luke (3:41–52). The whole event echoes the descent of the first Adam into a fleshly vehicle. Jesus of Nazareth, soon to receive a higher Being from the spiritual world at his baptism by John, is seen to counterpoise the first Adam's relegation to the earthly world below. The element of reversed correspondence is evident in that it was the first Adam's deeds which landed him in matter, whereas the newly arriving second Adam from on high voluntarily descended into the meticulously prepared physical body of Jesus of Nazareth, who descended from the first Adam, thus regularizing the whole affair.

More significant correspondences

The principle of reversed correspondences continues in the 'temptations' phenomenon. The first Adam (and Eve, of course) fell victim to the temptations of the Devil and thereby allowed Satan to do his work in the form of introducing the principle of death. The opposing principles of earthly life and death were thereby established. Lucifer, the Light-bearer, was instrumental in bringing 'enlightenment' to Adam and Eve, as a result of their eating the fruit of the Tree of Knowledge of Good and Evil.

At this point the actual transfer of abode for Adam and Eve occurs, and life on the earthly realm commences. 'And made Yahweh Elohim for man and for his wife tunics of skin, and caused to put on them' (Genesis 3:21). Interestingly enough, in verse 17 we read: '. . . cursed (is) the ground for the sake of thee; in sorrow shalt thou eat (of) it all (the) days of thy lives.' (It may be significant that the plural *lives* is employed, for humankind is being condemned henceforth to a series of lives stretching far into the future.) It was pointed out earlier in Genesis 3:16: 'Unto the woman he (Yahweh Elohim) said: Causing to be great I will cause to be great thy sorrow and thy conception; in pain shalt thou bring forth sons, and unto thy husband thy desire and he shall rule in (or over) thee.' This upholds the notion that mankind, spiritual beings all, are obliged to inhabit a material body, their whole existence being divided between heaven and earth: birth into the material world and death to the spiritual world alternating with death to the spiritual realms and birth into the physical. Significantly perhaps, the actual word 'death' is not mentioned in connection with all this, and there is every justification for positing that the process is one of ever-continuing metamorphosis rather than any *end* as such.

It would not be exaggerating and is certainly in accord with reason to argue that we human beings were born out of the cosmos into the earth—this is the correct sequence. The Zohar refers to Adam and Eve being clothed in garments of light whilst in the Garden of Eden. Certainly, we did not originate from the earth, as orthodox scientific thinking maintains, but from the heavens. This is made plain in Genesis 2:1, 'Thus the heavens and the earth were finished, and the host of them,' and only after this was the shift made by Adam and Eve from the heavens to the earth in the shape of the Fall. The references to 'dust' uphold the actuality that Adam and Eve's earthly existence commenced with their expulsion from the garden of Eden; but prior to that they inhabited the heavenly realms as purely spiritual beings. A literal rendering of Genesis 3:19 runs: 'In sweat of thy nostrils, shalt thou eat bread, until thy return unto the ground; for from her (it) wast thou taken; for dust (art) thou, and unto dust thou shalt return.'

In the case of the newly baptized Christ Jesus, a similar scenario arises: the second Adam was also subjected to temptations, again by the Devil and Satan. The Lord's Prayer has us saying, 'And lead us not into temptation; but deliver us from evil,' or 'that which is evil, or the evil (one)' (Matthew 6:13; Luke 11:4). This 'spirit of evil' is none other than Satan (*Satanas*), and here the use of the definite article validates reference to an actual being or entity rather than to 'evil' as an abstraction. Satan, Ahriman, bringer of obstacles, hindrances and frustrations, and the god of death itself, was declared by Zarathustra to be the enemy of Ormuzd, the Creator of the World, and the source of goodness and light—who else but the Christ Being?

Similarly, 'temptation' does not refer to an abstraction, but rather to the Devil (*Diabolos*). In general, however, both the Devil and Satan are considered as demonic and devilish. The designations Lucifer and Ahriman are, in effect, collective nouns applied respectively to all spiritual beings of diabolic or satanic nature. In Zoroastrian times, Ahriman was regarded as the spirit of darkness and—by inference—evil, whose antagonist was Ahura Mazda as representative of light and goodness. However, Lucifer must not be actually identified with Ahura Mazda, but instead regarded as light-bearer (as his name infers) rather than light-giver.

Rudolf Steiner often pointed out that it is always prudent to be alert to the presence of the artistic element to be detected in both the Old and New Testament Scriptures. We have already noted that the first Adam had no parentage other than God himself, and neither did Eve. In Genesis 2:21–4 we read that she was made from one of Adam's ribs; this is a typical case of the principle of reversal, one becoming two. As for 'the book of the generations of Adam' at Genesis 5:1–2,

Eve is not mentioned by name; rather, 'male and female called he (God) them, and blessed them, and called *their* name Adam'. This, therefore, is a parallel case of 'one becoming two', and in a certain sense echoes the 'making' of the second Adam by the event whereby the individuality of the Matthew Jesus passed over into the Luke Jesus at about the age of twelve. True to type in the sense of reversal or counterpoise, *the two became one.*

It is significant that Christ Jesus as second Adam was to be put to temptation, as was the first Adam, and this immediately after his baptism by John (Matthew 4:1–11; Mark 1:13; Luke 4:2–14). (In this respect it is hardly facetious to point out that had the Christ Being been 'born' as a child, he would surely have suffered many temptations before the age of 30 or so, when his baptism took place.) This sequence of events supports the Adoptionist contention, namely, that the Christ Being was as it were 'born' at the moment that the Holy Spirit—represented descending in the shape of a dove—entered into the body of Jesus of Nazareth. Luke places his account immediately after his list of ancestors right up to God himself (Luke 3:38), after declaring (3:22–3) that the newly baptized Jesus was indeed his Son. The 'voice from heaven', as reported in the texts of all three Synoptic Gospels, declared that the newly baptized Jesus of Nazareth was his 'beloved Son, in whom he was 'well pleased'.

At Acts 13:33 we read: 'God hath fulfilled the same (promise) unto us their (fathers') children, in that he raised Jesus again; as it is also written in the second Psalm (verse 7), 'Thou art my Son, this day have I begotten thee.' In this respect it will be recalled that Acts was written by Luke, and that its wording in most Bibles concerning the baptism runs: 'Thou art my beloved Son; in thee I am well pleased.' However, it bears repetition that some Bibles, e.g. the New English Bible, warn that 'some witnesses' maintain the wording that appears in Acts and Psalms, and also in Hebrews, and not that which appears in Matthew ('This is my beloved Son, in whom I am well pleased') and Mark ('Thou art my beloved Son, in whom I am well pleased').

The New English Bible is careful to note that 'Some witnesses read *My Son art thou, this day I have begotten thee.*' The proof-text of this rendering is to be found in Psalms 2:7, where the New English Bible has: 'You are my son,' he said; 'this day I become your father.' This statement is quoted by Luke in Acts 13:33, and further support for this Adoptionist view appears in the letter to the Hebrews (1:5; 5:5). All this carries the distinct message that Luke was a thoroughgoing Adoptionist. It is also worth pointing out that these particular letters (to the Hebrews) were not written by Paul, as commonly recorded in the Authorized Version and other translations (the basis for this conjecture being its suspiciously Pauline undertones) but probably by his collaborator Barnabas.

Paul the initiate

Rudolf Steiner averred that there can be little doubt that Paul was a pupil of initiates in the Mysteries, and that his firm conviction that the sublime Sun Being was to be found only in the heavenly world made him an enthusiastic opponent of the new Christianity. But when Paul had an encounter on the earthly plane, whom he realized was also the Sun Being, the shock was so great that he was rendered sightless for three days. When he had recovered with the help of Ananias he was firmly convinced that the man Jesus was indeed the Christ-

bearer, realizing that this same Being was the Sun Being of
Mystery teachings who had now united himself with the
earth. Paul's strange conversion threw the Jewish community
into confusion and bewilderment; they plotted to kill him, but
he escaped by being let down the city walls in a basket.

The well-known 'Damascus experience' underwent by Paul
was uncommon in that his conversion was so swift. In fact he
was incapacitated for three days—the usual length of time
taken by candidates for 'initiation' or 'enlightenment' in the
Mystery Centres—during which time he would have been
unaware of the material world but conscious in the spiritual
world. Upon his recovery he presented a greatly changed
character who was able to draw on his extensive knowledge of
the Jewish Scriptures and the Law. The reference in Acts 13:2
to the special mission of Paul and Barnabas and frequent
mention of their being filled with the Holy Spirit is indicative
of increasing powers and firmer confidence as a result of their
spiritual advancement.

Paul knew about the mysticism of heavenly ascents and
similar notions, which are echoed in the Cairo Damascus
Document. The ascents to the higher heaven tradition
through various degrees to 'Lesser Palaces' and 'Greater
Palaces' are mentioned in the *hekhalot* or *merkabah* literature,
and there was also a wealth of better known Gnostic and
other esoteric writings. Robert Reisenman, in *James the
Brother of Jesus,* contended that traditions about James and
his teachings were in accord with this kind of mystic tradition
and the idea of ascending via the Holy Spirit to the higher
spheres. An example of this kind of experience is mentioned
by Paul himself: 'I knew a man in Christ fourteen years ago,
(whether in the body, I cannot tell; or whether out of the
body, I cannot tell: God knoweth;) such an one caught up to

the third heaven' (II Corinthians 12.2). This statement he repeats in the very next verse.

Jesus was surprised, and somewhat scathing, when Nicodemus, 'a ruler of the Jews', appeared so dense about being 'born again' (John 3:7). This remark may with justification seem to apply to the 'virgin birth' of the 'higher self' from the lower. As Christ remarked, 'That which is born of the flesh is flesh: and that which is born of spirit is spirit' (John 3:6), and unless this occurs one cannot enter into the kingdom of God.

His further remark on the same occasion seems to have escaped all those early Church worthies who argued so earnestly about the nature of Christ Jesus: 'If I have told you earthly things, and ye believe not, how shall ye believe, if I tell you of heavenly things? And no man hath ascended up to heaven, but that he came down from heaven, even the Son of man which is in heaven' (John 3:12 13). More assurances are to be found in the so-called Gospel of Thomas (81:10–14): 'Jesus said: Know what is hidden before your face, and what is hidden from you will be revealed to you: for there is nothing hidden which will not be manifest.' Further confirmation may be found at Matthew 10:26, Mark 4:22 and Luke 8:17.

Epiphanius said of the 'Jews poor in spirit' known as the Ebionites: 'For some say Christ is Adam, the First created ... and is a Spirit higher than the Angels and Lord of all ... He comes here when he chooses, as when he came in Adam ... He came also in the Last Days, put on Adam's body, appeared to men, was crucified, resurrected, and ascended ... but also they say ... the Spirit which is Christ came into him and put on the man who is called Jesus.' (The 'Last Days' referred to here are those of the Old Covenant or Testament, for the whole Christ Event was already anticipated by the Mysteries, for he came to 'make all things new'.)

The pristine nature of the second Adam

It is certain that Paul was well acquainted with Mystery teachings, as evidenced by his knowledge of the two Adams. He knew very well that the soul of the second Adam, unsullied and undefiled in every respect, was incarnated *for the very first time* in the Luke Jesus. This 'second Adam-soul', as Rudolf Steiner described him, was indeed none other than the Luke Jesus, he who was totally inexperienced in earthly ways, but was a gentle, loving child, innocent of all tarnish and guile. On several medieval paintings such innocence and naivety is depicted by the inclusion in them of a boy counting on his fingers, apparently being prompted by a helpful lad of similar age—obviously representing the worldly-wise Matthew Jesus.

After a detailed preamble, Paul gets down to explaining the first Adam and the second Adam thus (I Corinthians 15:45–9): 'And so it is written, The first man Adam was made a living soul; the last Adam was made a quickening spirit. Howbeit that was not first that was spiritual, but that which is natural; and afterward what is spiritual. The first man is of the earth, earthy; the second man is the Lord from heaven. As is the earth earthy, such are they also that are earthy: and as is the heavenly, such are they also that are heavenly. And as we have borne the image of the earthy, we shall also bear the image of the heavenly.'

The whole of humanity suffered the 'Fall' by reason of their archetypal forebears 'eating of the Tree of the knowledge of good and evil'. This meant that Adam and Eve, our very progenitors, had by their disobedience thereby rendered themselves unworthy of partaking of the Tree of Life also. According to Steiner's interpretation of this legendary event, which was explained in his course of lectures in *The Gospel of St Luke*:

a portion of the etheric body (or life-body) was kept back and did not pass on to his [Adam's] descendants. In other words, this was the Adam-soul still untouched by human guilt and not yet entangled in the events whereby humanity suffered the Fall. These primeval Adam-forces were preserved, and existed until being conducted, as a 'provisional ego', to the child born to the Luke Joseph and Mary. Thus, in his early years, this Jesus-child had within him the unexpended power of the original prototype of earthly humanity, and at the appropriate time appeared in the form of the Luke Jesus. Paul was aware of this, and knowledge of it is concealed behind his words. His eventual pupil and helper, the writer of the Gospel of Luke, knew it too. Hence he gives Joseph a lineage extending back to Adam, who issued directly from the spiritual world and therefore, in Luke's language, was 'born of God'.

Thus Luke does this by tracing in his genealogy the ancestral line of ascent right up to the Creator—God himself—and lays stress on this notion by having the boy Jesus descending from (the first) Adam, and stating on the occasion of the temple incident that he was 'about his Father's business' (Luke 3:38; 2:49).

Paul knew about the pristine nature of the first Adam prior to his Fall into earthly conditions, and of the second Adam, whose soul was pure and undefiled. He also declared Christ Jesus to be 'the image of the invisible God, and the firstborn of every creature; for by him were all things created, that are in heaven, and that are in earth, visible and invisible...' (Colossians 1:15), thus echoing the first few verses of John's Gospel. According to the more esoteric traditions among the Church Fathers, the Logos had been 'shining in darkness', 'kept secret', 'hidden'. It is not difficult to detect the connections between the first Adam, exiled to the earthly realm at an indeterminate time after its creation, and the pre-existent Logos, characterized by Paul as the second Adam, whose mission to earth was to redeem Adam and his descendants from the result of the Fall. The traditional connections between sin and matter are also readily seen, as both were regarded as evil.

It is important to differentiate between the circumstances that precede both the Luke Jesus and the Matthew Jesus. In effect, the Luke Jesus had been 'reserved' in the spiritual worlds ever since the time of the original 'Adam and Eve', namely, during the Lemurian epoch, which immediately preceded the Atlantean civilization. In Enoch 48:3 we read: 'Before the sun and signs were created, before the stars were made, his name (the Messiah) was named before the Lord,' and 'he hath been chosen and hidden before him before the creation of the world' (Enoch 48:6).

By contrast, the individuality that was born to the Matthew parents had accumulated over hundreds of reincarnations, latterly from Abraham through David to the Matthew Joseph. This soul was therefore worldly-wise and seasoned, with considerable experience of life and conditions in the terrestrial realms, whereas the Luke child's soul was innocent and pure in every way, and positively deserving of all the qualities attaching to the entirely appropriate word *hagion,* as mentioned earlier.

Steps in approaching the Christ

Christ Jesus said: 'Come unto me, all ye that labour and are heavy laden, and I will give you rest. Take my yoke upon you, and learn of me; for I am meek and lowly in heart: and ye shall find rest unto your souls' (Matthew 15:28, 29). This exalted Being is a member of the spiritual hierarchy *Exousiai* (Powers or Authorities), who once sojourned on the earth in the bodily vehicle provided for him in the form of Jesus of Nazareth; he is still closely associated with the earth, but actually in the etheric sphere which encompasses it. Christ Jesus describes himself as 'descending from heaven' (John 6:38), and this can be fairly construed as coming 'from above', namely, the starry worlds which canopied the flat earth of biblical times. The literal translation of Matthew 28:18 runs '. . . has been given to me all authority (*exousia*) in heaven and on earth', followed at 28:20 by 'And lo, I am with you all the days until the completion of the age' (*aionos*— aeon, rather than 'world' as in the some Bibles).

This means that the now resurrected Christ may be found only in these 'heavenly' etheric realms, and is to be approached there. The will to take the first step on this road of spiritual advancement is the main prerequisite, and if progress is to be made this will-power must be strong enough to make the necessary changes in the life of soul and spirit, which inevitably engages the body also. There should be no need to labour such changes, but in this respect Christ Jesus had this to say: 'No man can come to me, except the Father which hath sent me draw him: and I will raise him up at the last day' (John 6:44). However, 'Jesus said unto him (Thomas), I am the way, the truth and the life: no man cometh unto the Father, but by me' (John 14:6). The Son is

saying this, and his status as 'LORD God' (Yahweh) befits
the meaning of this Name as 'The Existing One' to whom the
rest of us, as partakers in Creation, owe our very existence
(John 1:3). The Christ makes no demands and lays down no
laws, except that we love our neighbours as ourselves (Levi-
ticus 19:16; Galatians 5:14; James 2:8).

The very word 'father' has so many meanings, applications
and interpretations that the context in which it is used must
always be carefully considered from designating God, the
Godhead, Great All-embracing Spirit, Providence and so on
as Supreme Being which has no equal. This word invariably
bears connotations of certain beings or entities that are
comparatively senior and perhaps superior to whom they
minister. Its usage among most Mystery and organized
'received' religions is characterized by leaders rather than led,
teachers rather than taught, and holy (in the literal sense of
being separate) rather than profane. Absolute supremacy,
and furthest separation, was accorded by Christ to God the
Father, as guide and ruler of all Creation.

However, as 'sons' of 'the Father', or 'children of God' we
may be said to have 'issued' from him in the very first
instance, but we have been separated from him by the Fall.
This propensity, which is present in all human beings who
possess the yearning, so to speak, to 'return' by striving
towards our 'Holy Father' from whom we emanated, is
entirely inborn. This urge to identify with this higher or
superior entity is reflected in the universal practice of vener-
ating 'the best at . . .' in society and culture in general. There is
only one superlative, and that must be God himself. Earthly,
minor 'gods' strive to shed their comparative status, so we
have 'world champions' of every imaginable kind. Those who
reach the zenith of their particular field of endeavour become

'celebrities' or 'stars'. Most people envy such individuals, their fame and their fortune, and dearly wish to be like them, and receive the adoration of worshippers who confer it with all the fervour of religious zeal. This primal yearning to 'unite' with their success and enjoy the status it brings is, needless to say perhaps, rooted in egotism. Such heroes and their idolizers are invariably materialistic and earthbound; and as for the also-rans—well, there's always the lottery.

On the other hand, Scripture says, 'God is a Spirit: and they who worship him must worship him in spirit and in truth' (John 4:24). As has been vouchsafed all along, we humans are primarily spiritual beings, and only secondarily are we beings of flesh and blood. It is therefore perfectly right and proper that we seek whatever is of the spirit, and 'work out our own salvation with fear and trembling. For it is God which worketh both to will and to do his good pleasure' (Philippians 2:12–13). There is no shortage of hopefuls who, with all the earnestness and fervour of the medieval mystic, seek to return to their very source in the Godhead. As we know, however, the route to this source is to be reached only by way of the Son, Christ Jesus himself, the purveyor of grace and truth (John 1:14).

It is reasonable to postulate that this is the second step, the first being via the Holy Spirit: 'He (the Son) shall baptize you with the Holy Ghost, and with fire' (Matthew 3:11; Mark 1:8; Luke 3:16; John 1:33). Thus we have all four Evangelists declaring that those who aspire to spiritual heights shall first be baptized by none other than the Holy Spirit. We read that 'baptism with the Holy Spirit' is promised to the apostles (Acts 1:5), and at 1:8 that they 'shall receive power, after that the Holy Spirit is come upon (them)...' as happened at the time of Pentecost (Acts 2:1–4). Ideally, it is only after such a 'baptism of fire' by the agency of the Holy Spirit that the first step may be taken.

The event of Pentecost was preceded by 'a sound from heaven as of a rushing mighty wind (*pnoes biaias*—literally, 'violent breath'), and so somewhat reminiscent of *pneuma* (air in motion, wind, vital spirit) as in *pneuma hagion* (spirit holy) of the annunciation event at Luke 1:35). It almost seems that Luke is trying to associate these two events, applying the highly symbolic language sometimes employed by other New Testament contributors. The Holy Spirit was present at the 'heralding' of the Matthew Jesus at his birth, and also at his ascension—entry into the material world and departure therefrom into the etheric one.

We have now arrived at the point where a valid connection can be made from our present constitution in terms of physical-material, etheric and astral members to their counterparts in terms of soul and spirit. We all have the potential to develop the higher principles from the lower, and this is accomplished by means of exerting our supreme purely spiritual principle in the form of our ego. Now the youngest, nearest and thus most accessible principle to the ego is the astral body, and by means of *katharsis* there is the potential to develop from it a pure and morally 'higher' entity which Steiner called by its oriental appellation *Manas*, and which he later gave the term (anglicized as) *Spirit Self*. In considering these technicalities, it is again worth quoting Steiner, who during a lecture course *The Gospel of St John* given in Hamburg during May 1908 said:

This cleansed, purified astral body, which bears within it at the moment of illumination none of the impure impressions of the physical world, but only the organs of perception of the spiritual world, is called in esoteric Christianity the 'pure, chaste, wise Virgin Sophia'. By means of all that he receives during *katharsis*, the pupil cleanses and purifies his astral body so that it is transformed into the Virgin Sophia. And when the Virgin Sophia encounters the Cosmic Ego, the Universal Ego which causes illumination, the pupil is surrounded by light, spiritual light. This second power that approaches the Virgin Sophia is called in esoteric Christianity—and is also called today—the 'Holy Spirit'. Therefore, according to esoteric Christianity, it is correct to say that through his processes of initiation the Christian esotericist attains the purification and cleansing of his astral body; he makes his astral body into the Virgin Sophia and is illuminated from above—if you wish, you may call it overshadowed—by the 'Holy Spirit', by the Cosmic, Universal Ego.

It requires little reflection to conclude that the Luke Mary was so spiritually advanced that she, during the visitation of the angel at the Annunciation, attained the state of illumination at the 'coming upon' by the Holy Spirit and was made worthy of being regarded as 'Virgin Sophia'. After a little more cogitation it becomes reasonable to contend that the controversies regarding 'virgin birth', 'virginal conception' and similar notions were as it were 'materialized' by those who saw fit to externalize the whole event. This is understandable, for the task of making such esoteric or 'hidden' truths clear to the unprepared masses simply would be neither feasible nor desirable. But clues of these deeper meanings and implications seem to have been deliberately sprinkled by the Synoptic Evangelists, Matthew, Mark and Luke, as exemplified elsewhere, whereas John's Gospel is richly laced with esoteric truths.

So here we have an answer to the whole 'virgin birth' controversy. By construing it in spiritual rather than material terms, seeming nonsense has given way to seeing matters as they really are—when they make perfect sense. That the whole matter was 'externalized' by reifying it for the sake of the faithful masses in a manner they could understand seemed a good idea at the time. This idea has lasted for almost two thousand years, and the time has inevitably arrived when mere belief had to become insufficient and therefore unsatisfactory. Just as the earth was found not to be flat, and that our planet revolves around the sun and not vice versa, so we are able to understand the real facts behind the enigma of the two clearly set out genealogies of Matthew and Luke, and the reasons for their incompatibilities.

Our threefold soul and spirit members

Just as we are threefold in our bodily or corporeal constitution, so are we similarly threefold in our soul nature and threefold in our spiritual nature (see Chapter 2). This gives a ninefold model of ourselves which is entirely valid:

Spiritual members	Spirit Self	Life Spirit	Spirit Man
Soul members	Sentient soul	Intellectual soul	Consciousness soul
Corporeal members	Astral body	Etheric body	Physical body

Nowadays, of these nine principles only the physical body is acknowledged as 'real'. Where the etheric body is concerned, there is talk of 'force-fields', 'morphic fields' and the like. An 'astral body' of some kind is claimed by some to be visible, but whatever claims are made it is quite impossible for astral 'substance' to be apprehended by our bodily senses. Those aspirants who undergo *katharsis*, the cleansing of the astral body, thus activating their sentient soul and Spirit Self in that they became capable of supersensory perception in the spiritual world, and thus 'full of the Holy Spirit', were said in the language of esoteric Christianity to have transformed their astral body into the 'Virgin Sophia'. This is a profoundly esoteric concept, more of which can be found in the self-evident titles that appear in the Bibliography.

With reference to the table below, it may seem odd that what is usually regarded as our coarsest, least spiritual principle should constitute the basis of our most highly developed supersensible member. It is, however, the oldest and 'most perfect' of the three, as its progression may be traced back to the evolutionary stage known as Old Saturn. Accordingly, our etheric body was acquired during the Old Sun stage; our astral body, bestowed during the Old Moon stage, is the 'youngest' of the three and therefore, in evolutionary terms, the least perfect. Contrariwise, our astral nature is the closest in character to the power of our ego, and therefore most accessible in terms of influence. When the astral body has been purified after undergoing *katharsis* it is transformed into its spiritual function as Spirit Self, the stage that Steiner called Imagination. This principle equates, as we have seen, with the Holy Spirit, the oriental term for which is Manas. Similarly, when the ego has succeeded in transforming the etheric body, the corresponding spiritual entity is designated Life Spirit or Budhi, its stage of spiritual development being that of Inspiration. And by the same token Spirit Man is known as Atman in oriental terms, and Intuition by Steiner, thus:

Astral	Spirit Self	Manas	Mysteries of the Holy Spirit (Imagination)
Etheric	Life Spirit	Budhi	Mysteries of the Son (Inspiration)
Physical	Spirit Man	Atman	Mysteries of the Father (Intuition)

The conditions required for anyone embarking on the first stage in the form of the Mysteries of the Holy Spirit are demanding in terms of purity of soul, which means that the undertaking of *katharsis* may not be lightly undertaken. At Hebrews 10:32 we read: 'But call to remembrance the former days, in which, after ye were illuminated, ye endured a great fight of afflictions...' which take many forms. Jesus himself gives warning at Luke 9:62: 'No man, having put his hand to the plough, and looking back, is fit for the kingdom of God.'

Such warnings were echoed by Rudolf Steiner, without doubt the most proficient of seers in modern times, who discusses how such knowledge may be attained in his book *Knowledge of the Higher Worlds,* further amplified by *The Way of Self-knowledge* and *Stages of Higher Knowledge*, all of which are meticulous in the presentation of their contents. In the latter book he discusses and advises on these stages, namely, Imagination, Inspiration and Intuition, which approximate to the three levels of spiritual perception described concerning the development of Spirit Self, Life Spirit and Spirit Man respectively, as tabulated above. It must be understood that there is no hint of gurus, 'Masters' or suchlike in any of these books. Steiner makes this absolutely clear, remarking that they should rather be regarded as representing a dialogue between the reader as novice and himself as teacher, spiritual researcher and investigator. They contain descriptions of the kind of exercises necessary for undertaking what is a very demanding assignment, the essential prerequisites for which being a strong will, patience and perseverance. Needless to say, perhaps, the rewards are many in terms of spiritual development as well as being both emotionally and intellectually satisfying.

In these books there is no mention whatever of Christ or Christianity; they map out the ways of accessing the spiritual worlds in strictly neutral terms, i.e. by means of meditation pure and simple, which will fit any kind of faith or belief that is genuinely spiritual in nature and content. This is not to say that he himself was not a Christian: his book *Christianity as Mystical Fact* appeared in 1902, and he made public his Christology during the first decade or so of the twentieth century—despite the fact that he was Secretary-General of the Theosophical Society during this period. However, it was because of his disagreement with Annie Besant, the then leader of the Theosophical Society, with regard to her claims that Jiddu Krishnamurti was the reincarnated Christ. Steiner declared that Christ Jesus could be incarnated once, and once only, and in the series of lectures on the Gospels and Christianity in general he developed a whole Christology, which he continually extended until his death in March 1925. Throughout his life Steiner maintained that his system of spiritual science, based on the investigatory standards and methods of material science, set out to describe things *as they are* and not what they are *believed to be*.

A way forward

The first stage of spiritual development is that of producing the Spirit Self from the astral body, and it demands that all self-seeking be eliminated from the soul. This process is not normally an instantaneous event, but rather a gradual process of transformation. In this respect the factor of metamorphosis is involved in that the 'substance' comprising the astral body is spiritualized by the agency of the ego, and this allows the steady development of the Spirit Self from our sentient soul, which warrants the employment of the term *Holy Spirit* to characterize it. At the same time individuals seeking spiritual advancement will assist such transmutation by strengthening their propensity for pouring forth their capacity for a *love* that is unconditional and universal in the sense of *agape*. In one of the meditations given by Steiner appears the line: 'The godhood of my soul outpours in purest love to all that is,' which is indicative of this.

This, in a few words, confirms our spiritual nature, accentuates the fact that love flows from an inexhaustible source, guarantees its unalloyed quality, and calls for this most precious of all gifts to be bestowed on the whole of Creation. And also this is in full accord with his notion of humanity's ranking in the spiritual Hierarchies as Spirits of Love and Freedom. Steiner often referred to love as being 'the moral Sun of the World', with its spiritual origins traceable back to God, and indeed the Christ also. Paul, at II Corinthians 6:6, not unexpectedly says very much the same when he calls upon his collaborators to commend themselves (6:4) 'By pureness, by knowledge, by kindness, by the Holy Spirit, by love unfeigned.'

As the attainment to the ability to embrace 'all that is' in purest love brings the ability to access the Mysteries of the Holy Spirit and attain sufficient transmutation of the astral body to bring about the formation of the Spirit Self by the deployment of universal love, so the eradication of all untruthfulness allows the aspirant to approach the Mysteries of the Son by embracing truth, thus bringing about the power of creating Life Spirit from our Intellectual Soul, which is founded in our etheric body. This renders it sufficiently mature for Christ as 'Son' to 'bring never ceasing revelations' to sincere individuals who persevere. Paul, at II Corinthians 6:7 continues, 'By the word of truth, by the power of God, by the armour of righteousness on the right hand and on the left,' thus encouraging his helpers also to commend themselves. This injunction was made earlier in the letter (4:2): (We have) 'renounced the hidden things of dishonesty, not walking in craftiness, nor handling the word of God deceitfully; but by manifestation of the truth by commending ourselves to every man's conscience in the sight of God.' Emphasis on the desirability—the necessity even—of upholding what is true is everywhere to be found in the Scriptures. John's epistle at I:3:18 reads, 'My little children, let us not love in word, neither in tongue: but in deed and in truth,' thus nicely brings these two essential moral qualities together as does Paul at Ephesians 4:15 by extolling 'the speaking of truth in love'. Steiner, as might be expected, also connects these two factors within a meditational verse:

The seed of Truth lives in Love,
In Truth seek the root of Love:
Thus speaks thy higher Self . . .

The principle of Spirit Self is rooted in our etheric nature and is gradually formed from the intellectual or mind soul, thereby allowing access to the Mysteries of the Son. This stage is called Inspiration in the language of spiritual science. It is noteworthy that, as indicated earlier, the Christ Being was traditionally associated with the sun. As mentioned earlier, he is now as it were resident in the etheric world, the realm of the Hierarchy of Angels.

The present stage of human development is that of the consciousness soul, which is related to Spirit Self on the one hand and our physical-material organization on the other. This circumstance is in accordance with evolutionary laws as being normal. The third stage, namely, the Mysteries of the Father as Creator of humanity itself, has to do with the working over by our ego of the secrets of our near-perfect physical-material body, thus to produce within ourselves the principle of Spirit Man. By earnest, honest toil it is already possible for individuals to attain to the stage of Spirit Man, and therefore Intuition.

This universal transmutation of the consciousness soul into Spirit Man is not due to begin until the time allotted, which will be many centuries hence.

Developing our latent powers

As representing our supreme spiritual constituent, the ego may not, strictly speaking, be designated a 'member' *per se*, for it never leaves the spiritual world in which it is ensconced. It is so powerful that it is capable of purifying and ennobling every other constituent, whether astral, etheric, material or spiritual in nature, to the point of perfection, at the same time preparing itself for further tasks. It must always be borne in mind that the principle of evolution is a cosmic law, to which even the spiritual hierarchies themselves are subject. One of the many purposes of evolving humankind as resident on our similarly evolving planet earth is, according to Rudolf Steiner, for human beings to introduce and practise their faculties and develop their potentialities for the exercise of love and freedom. This profound proposition is rooted deeply in what is now ranked as esoteric wisdom and knowledge, but which will in future developmental epochs come to fruition, with the prospect of even further stages on the path to perfection. Absolute perfection is the prerogative of the ineffable Godhead as Great All-encompassing Spirit only, which at present is still only partly subject to full apprehension.

6
PROBLEMS WITH THE TWO MARYS

*Then one said to him, Behold, thy mother and thy brethren
stand without, desiring to speak with thee. But he answered
and said unto him that told him, Who is my mother? Who
are my brethren? And he stretched forth his hand towards
his disciples, and said, Behold my mother and my brethren.*
Matthew 12:47–9

Who are the real heretics?

Whoever is bold enough to tackle the manifold problems
concerning the biblical 'Mary' (or more correctly both of the
two Marys who gave birth to a boy called Jesus as proclaimed
in the Bible) does so with considerable trepidation. Whatever
is said is certain to be challenged by whatever organized
Christian church authority, not to mention those who
repudiate the matter entirely. Throughout the last 15 or more
centuries the orthodox belief has persisted that the mother of
Jesus—or Christ, perhaps—was the Mary cited by Luke in his
Gospel. His Mary has come to be recognized as *the Mary*,
that is to say, 'the Virgin Mary', and this in spite of biblical
evidence that the Mary mentioned in Matthew's Gospel also
gave birth to a boy named Jesus at around the same time, and
that both mothers were virginal. In short, Christian teachings
as they have unfolded over time emerge as unequivocally
wrong and the Bible they are built on as glaringly right.

The present ways of thinking and perceiving were very
different from those obtaining two millennia ago; then they

were imaginative and symbolic rather than intellectual and actual, and conditioned by preconceptions and entrenched attitudes resulting from the various beliefs acquired by means of the particular socialization of each individual. The inevitable consequence is that most Christians simply had, and still have, to rely on what they are told to believe by those in authority in the various denominations and sects. The simplistic notion that the spirit is somehow good and the body evil widely prevailed. The observation—or supposition turned fact—that both Mary and her son Jesus remained 'virginal' all their lives, in spite of the fact that other family members are often mentioned in the New Testament, was frequently quoted as endorsing the desirability of following a monastic life of celibacy. It is probable that there are much more profound reasons for placing emphasis on the whole concept, not only of virginity as such but on an archetypal image of that which brings forth something utterly new. The notion of virgin birth certainly had a very deep meaning within the Mystery Schools. For essentially the birth of our 'higher self' in the soul is indeed a 'virgin birth', that of the 'Christ in me' in the Pauline sense—of which more later.

The Theotokos dispute

The commonly held belief by some factions, namely, that Mary was the Mother of God (*Theotokos*) presents many and prominent difficulties of its own. Rather than 'Mother of God', the rendering '(who) gave birth to God' is more apt. The 'Virgin Mary' was proclaimed *Theotokos* at the Council of Ephesus in 431, the notion of virgin motherhood being first proclaimed at the First Council of Constantinople. Anastasius, a fifth-century theologian, declared: 'Let no one call

Mary *Theotokos*, for Mary was the mother of the human nature only, and it is impossible that God should be born of a woman!' The most common objection was then, and is now, that if Christ as the *Logos* or Word is the creator of all things, how can he be described as a creature of that which he himself created? As Nestorius, the heretic Church Father said: 'Just imagine—a three-year-old child as Creator of the world!' It is absolutely impossible to claim that Christ, as Logos, was in any way 'conceived' or 'born'. Spiritual beings can never be 'born' in the ordinary sense of the word, for they are incorporeal as well as immortal. By the same token, it is equally impossible for him—or perhaps more properly 'it', as the Christ Being has no gender—to have had a 'mother' except in the sense of metaphor and symbol. As an exalted spiritual being his ancestry stops at 'Father', but this term can only be symbolic.

It is more than likely that here we have the origins of the later beliefs concerning the Virgin Mary and her son Jesus; but it also guarantees its erroneousness. What was originally merely a symbol, a kind of visual aid for neophytes in the Mystery Schools, was in time reified, externalized as material reality, presenting what was in essence a prototype—as will be argued in due course. A pedant might justifiably argue that the representation of a 'virgin holding a child on her lap' would imply that the child could not, by sheer definition, be hers, but some other mother's, thus making a contradictory nonsense of everything. However, the use of this symbol as such would probably not have been misconstrued in those times, long before the onset of materialistic thinking.

There are, of course, grounds for involvement of the notion of virginity as such simply because our 'higher self' is produced out of our 'lower self' by reason of 'self-fertilization' by purely spiritual processes. The true meaning of the well-known exhortation 'Know thyself' which arose from the Mysteries as the epitome of Mystery-wisdom is manifold in application. Obviously, simple, straightforward self-knowledge in the biological, psychological and even spiritual senses is highly desirable. Through knowing ourselves thoroughly, as beings of spirit and soul as well as body, we come to know the Mysteries of both sensible and supersensible worlds. The age-old notion of ourselves as a microcosm which mirrors the macrocosm is a true one, as Steiner consistently demonstrates in his lectures published as *Mystery of the Universe, the Human Being, Image of Creation*.

Traditionalists will object that it cannot be doubted that the Incarnation did take place, but the Adoptionist position as argued in Chapter 1 is so little known because the 'establishment' in the shape of orthodox teachings did not then—as now—allow it. The dispute is not *that* it happened, but when. One undervalued element of the Incarnation mystery is that the pre-existent Logos, a Being who was not subject to the constraints of space and time, entered this temporal and spatial world of ours at all. Surely, it is reasonable to assert that as an exalted spiritual Being ranking far above ourselves it should scarcely be necessary for Christ Jesus to undergo all the experiences of childhood and youth and to experience the whole gamut of the human maturational processes. Son of God he may be, but not necessarily a 'son' in the purely human sense of being a male child. Few Christians would deny that the Christ, as the Logos, was (or is) pre-existent, and can in no sense be described as being 'born' or even created. John has him saying, 'Verily, verily, I say unto you, Before Abraham was, I am' (8:58), and there is no mistaking the emphasis: the Christ simply *is*. John's Gospel makes it clear that the Logos existed 'in the beginning' (1:2) and was truly pre-existent, a notion that has been largely ignored throughout centuries of Christian teaching.

The Churches have doggedly maintained that the Incarnation occurred at the time of the birth of Mary's son Jesus; accordingly, he was Jesus (the) Christ from the moment he was conceived. At the baptism in the Jordan he is said to have received the gift of the Holy Spirit, thereby commissioning him for his work. However, if the Trinity and its meaning and implications be taken seriously, could he not by virtue of his being cooperative with (as substance of) the Father and the Holy Spirit be deemed to be in possession of this latter principle already?

In all three Synoptic Gospels (Matthew 4:1; Mark 1:12; Luke 4:1), it is reported that Jesus was led, or driven 'of the Spirit into the wilderness', with Luke adding that he was full of the Holy Spirit. It is difficult to say what this particular 'Spirit' is; all three mention it without any qualification in terms of grammar, but the question remains as to why Luke differentiates between the Spirit and the Holy Spirit in the very same sentence. Jesus of Nazareth has just, in all three Gospels, been proclaimed by God (the Father) that he is (now) his Son, and by the terms of the Trinity must bear the principle of the Holy Spirit within him. One can only construe the plain word 'Spirit' in all three accounts as referring to the now indwelling Christ who has 'taken over' Jesus of Nazareth.

Virginal conception—fact or fancy?

The present argument posits that there were two Marys, two Josephs and two Jesus boys, but only one Jesus of Nazareth, as the Matthew boy died at about the age of twelve. It is necessary to bear in mind that when 'Mary' is mentioned, and unless otherwise stated, both Marys are being referred to up to and until the decease of the Luke Mary in what must have been her mid-twenties. As a rule, when orthodox Christians mention Mary, they are referring to the Luke Mary. As being comparatively less important, the two Josephs are usually identified in the text as and when necessary. Thus, the Incarnation is generally understood as having taken place at the time of conception by the agency of the Holy Spirit only, and without any male human involvement. This is the orthodox standpoint, a dogma which is widely accepted in spite of its many and obvious faults and deficiencies. A cogent example of this begs the question of the prominence given to the genealogies of the two Josephs if or when they are considered to have been unnecessary: they were not included to be ignored.

An opposing conviction maintains that the Christ was not in any sense conceived, but was 'born' in Jesus of Nazareth at his baptism in the River Jordan. This is an Adoptionist view, held by certain Church Fathers known as Nestorians, but has long since been regarded as unorthodox. However, arguments in support of it will follow in due course which strengthen the notion that the Incarnation did not take place at the birth of either the Matthew or the Luke Jesus.

The whole problem of the 'virgin birth', or more correctly the 'virginal conception' is extremely complex, but all the more worthy of close attention. That both Marys were virginal there is no doubt. There was no masculine element involved, if one leaves the Josephs out. The word 'Spirit', leaving out the adjective 'Holy' for the moment, is feminine in Hebrew (*ruach*) and neuter in Greek (*pneuma*). We must, therefore, dismiss from our minds anything with connotations of sex or insemination by any kind of sexual activity. Quite often in the apocryphal gospels Jesus Christ alludes to 'my mother the Holy Spirit', but there are other interpretations of such a statement.

The meticulous and discriminating biblical scholar Raymond Brown, in his book *The Birth of the Messiah*, states: 'There is no clear evidence of a virginal conception in any pregospel material other than the angelic annunciation of the anticipated birth.' He goes on to say: 'I came to the conclusion that the scientifically controllable evidence leaves the question of the historicity of the virginal conception unresolved ... and a resurvey of the evidence leaves me even more convinced of that.' He points out that the literal meaning of *en gastri* is 'having in the womb', and that there is no Greek substantive there either in Matthew 1:18 or at 1:20. At Matthew 1:18, the translation of the text where Mary 'was found with child' can lead to misunderstanding. He goes on, 'When one has supplied the word "child", the reading "child of the Holy Spirit" gives the false impression that the Holy Spirit is the father of the child. There is never a suggestion in Matthew or Luke that the Holy Spirit is the male element in a union with Mary, supplying the husband's role in begetting. Not only is the Holy Spirit not male (feminine in Hebrew; neuter in Greek), but also the manner of begetting is implicitly creative rather than sexual. The lack of the definite article (also missing in the parallel description of the pregnancy in Luke 1:35) tempts one to speak of "a Holy Spirit". The third person of the Trinity is not meant, as this theology had not yet been developed.'

Problems as to how translators construe the Greek text are numerous, and create enormous difficulties both for them and their dependent readers. It is demonstrable, in matters of interpretation errors and doubtful phraseology, that exegesis can all too easily become eisegesis, and serious mistakes have been made, as will be discussed.

As Brown avers, the reading 'of *the* Holy Spirit' gives the false impression that the Holy Spirit is the father of the child. It is noteworthy that some translators signify their uneasiness about this by placing the word 'the' in parentheses. Matthew is strangely repetitious concerning the whole affair, for at 1:23 he states the bare facts: 'Behold, the virgin shall be with child, and shall bring forth a son, and they shall call his name Emmanuel, which being interpreted is, God with us.' Such a statement certainly allows for the fatherhood by Joseph in the usual way. It is interesting to compare these considerations with reference to a parallel dilemma at Luke 1:35, which has other problems, some of which will be examined in due course.

There is also confusion in the minds of many people concerning the so-called Immaculate Conception, namely, the long-held belief that the Virgin Mary herself was conceived in such a fashion so as to be free of original sin and thus avoiding the corrupting influences of the flesh that could possibly be passed on to Jesus. This belief is often mistaken for the notion of the virgin birth, which is to do with the conception of Jesus or Christ, or both simultaneously as Jesus Christ, an event commonly referred to as the Incarnation.

The term 'virgin birth', is in any case a misnomer, for what most people usually mean when they speak of it is 'virginal conception'. Any arguments concerned with these notions are centred on the actual means and processes of conception; the actual birth itself is of no inherent interest. Similarly, any assertion that Mary (the two Marys, of course) was *virgo intacta* at the time of conception is also of little real concern, although in fact they were both virginal: the Matthew Mary (1:25) and the Luke Mary (2:7).

Some factions of the early Church were inordinately concerned with the notion of virginity, and so it has remained. Emphasis was placed on the 'fact' that Mary remained a virgin in spite of the birth process. In one of the several apocryphal gospels is the story of Salome, who, after the birth itself, made an attempt to discover whether Mary's hymen had been ruptured, and she suffered an injured hand and arm in the process, which, however, was immediately healed by a touch from the newborn baby. However, this kind of narrative attracts the kind of attention it deserves.

In those times virgin births were representative of union between the divine and human, which resulted in the birth of a god or superior being—in the language of symbol, the result of union of heaven and the earth. The Great Mother, Queen of Heaven, was a virgin, and her son was regarded as being born of the spirit or the will. Paradoxically enough, however, she was also regarded as being born of her own son, thereby symbolizing identity. Strange as this kind of language is to the modern mind, it would have been understood as intended in New Testament times. Significantly, this kind of thinking illustrates the dangers of preserving 'flat-earth' attitudes in our own time. In addition, the virginal conception element in the nativity accounts of both Matthew and Luke has led to a common hypothesis that the infancy stories represent a combination of different pre-gospel narratives and traditions. There is no clear evidence of any pre-Gospel material other than the angelic annunciation of the birth. As we shall see, the proof-text usually quoted in support of the virginal conception, namely, Isaiah 7:14, is open to serious doubt.

However, the creedal references to Jesus Christ being 'born of the Virgin Mary' that originated in the traditions of the Gospel nativity stories are still in place, regardless of the widespread personal conviction on the part of 'believers' that this assertion does not represent the actual material facts. The First Council of Constantinople in 381 proclaimed the virginal motherhood of Mary, who was duly declared *Theotokos* (Mother of God) at the Council of Ephesus in 431. Her attribute of 'ever-virgin' was accorded at the Council of Chalcedon in 451, and this became a dogma of the Church at the First Lateran Council in 649. That was then. In modern times, during the first half of the twentieth century, the *Report of the Commission on Christian Doctrine* appointed by the then Archbishops of Canterbury and York contains the following: 'Many of us hold ... that belief in the Word being made flesh is integrally bound up with belief in the Virgin Birth. There are, however, some among us who hold that a full belief in the historical Incarnation is more consistent with the supposition that our Lord's birth took place under normal conditions of human generation.'

Modern science, with its detailed knowledge of such matters, dismisses out of hand anything as miraculous as conception without the agency of a human father. Pleas to the effect that 'anything is possible with God', and that conformation with ordinary scientific laws in such a unique event as the virginal conception does not apply, do not signify to the majority of people. Many believers point out the consistency of Church teaching concerning the virginal conception from about 200 to about 1800, but this in itself means nothing more than a continuing lack of critical appraisal. Memories of 'heretical' Christians being burnt at the stake, the Inquisition and so on remained very much alive in historical memory—very potent factors in discouraging any kind of opposition to orthodoxy. Moreover, the effects of the Industrial Revolution and the inevitable growth of materialistic science and technology during the nineteenth century, not to mention Darwinism, spelt danger for the Churches of all persuasions, most of which have been in decline ever since.

More misconceptions concerning Mary

It is clear that the proof-text, if that is what Isaiah 7:14 is taken to be, rests on very shaky ground indeed. Taken in context, the verse is to do with a prophecy spoken by the Lord God himself to Ahaz, a king of Judah in the eighth century BC, after an aborted attempt to march on Jerusalem. It is foretold of the child Immanuel referred to by Isaiah that 'Butter and honey shall he eat, that he may know to refuse the evil and choose the good,' but before this happens, the land that Ahaz abhorred 'shall be forsaken of both her kings'. All this hardly seems to have much bearing on the circumstances attending the nativity stories.

However, much of the belief that Mary was a virgin relies on this proof-text at Isaiah 7:14: 'Therefore the Lord himself shall give you a sign; Behold, a virgin shall conceive, and bear a son, and shall call his name Immanuel.' In Hebrew, the word *almah*, which means simply a young woman of marriageable age, was translated into the Greek of the Septuagint as *parthenos*, used to designate a maiden or virgin, and employed by Matthew (1:23) and Luke (1:27). The reason for the choice of *parthenos* in the Septuagint is not known; in some later Greek versions of the Old Testament the word *almah* was translated as *neanis*—a young person. Strangely enough, *parthenos* was translated as 'damsel' (Authorized

Version) and 'girl' (New English Bible) to designate a female who was demonstrably not a virgin, as she had been 'defiled' by the local prince (Genesis 34:1–3). Interesting in this context is the fact that the New English Bible, at Isaiah 7:14, translated *almah* correctly—'young woman'. However, that same Bible has 'virgin' and 'girl' respectively for *parthenos* in Matthew 1:23 and Luke 1:27. Translators must have had their reasons, including deliberate eisegesis, but such practices should simply not be allowed to go unchallenged.

At Matthew 1:16 most texts speak plainly of Joseph as being the husband of Mary; some read, 'Jacob was the father of Joseph the husband of Mary, of whom was born Jesus, who is (now) called the Christ,' whilst others read, 'Joseph, to whom was betrothed the virgin Mary, who bore Jesus the Christ.' An Old Syriac text (Sinaiticus) reads: 'Jacob was the father of Joseph, to whom the virgin Mary was betrothed, was the father of Jesus who is called the Christ.' It is therefore a matter of taking one's pick of these. Certainly, there has been much speculation as to why such stress was laid by Matthew and Luke to portray their Marys as virginal, and naturally this warrants discussion.

In the case of Matthew, it is widely believed that his reason was to refute slanderous accusations to the effect that Jesus was of illegitimate birth, having been the issue of a liaison between Mary and a Roman soldier called Pantherus. Significant, too, is the inclusion in the Matthew genealogy of the four women of doubtful reputation, namely, Tamar, Rahab, Ruth and Bathsheba, all of whom were of non-Jewish extraction. It has been suggested that because of all this it would be prudent to emphasize the purity and chastity of Mary. However, virginity as such was not particularly highly valued by the Hebrews, and this adds weight to the notion that this element of the nativity stories was added later by the founders of the early Church in order to mollify those who believed that everything to do with 'the flesh' was evil, and that good was attachable only to spirit. This emphasis on virginity attained grotesque proportions within the thinking of the Roman Catholic Church, as history has shown.

Luke takes a more discreet—and acceptable—line, emphasizing by way of the annunciation and her coy reactions to it that Mary could be no other than a virgin. However, the emphasis is still there in the story, though this is lacking in the genealogies in both Gospels. In any case, both the Matthew Mary (1:25) and the Luke Mary (2:7) are reported to be virginal, and both Jesuses were firstborns. The tenacious grip that orthodox Christian doctrinal authorities have maintained over the centuries with regard to the virginity problem is now working to their detriment. As mentioned earlier, many biblical scholars maintain that these details were actually late additions to the birth stories. Jesus (of Nazareth) himself never referred to his birth, however remarkable or miraculous it was reputed to be. Neither, for that matter, did any member of his family, who might reasonably be expected to do so for similar reasons. It is not mentioned by anyone at all in the remainder of Matthew and Luke, nor in Mark, John, nor in any other New Testament book. Paul, in concert with all this, asserts in Galatians 4:4 that Jesus had been 'born (or made) of woman' in the ordinary way, and in this connection it is as well to remember that his letters pre-dated all the canonical Gospels, with the possible exception of Mark. It appears, then, that the case for virginal conception is seen, on close examination, to be woefully thin.

'Holy Family', believed to be by Bernart von Orley. Left to right: Matthew family, Luke family, Elizabeth with John.

Yet more complications

A serious complication concerns the annunciation to Mary at home in Nazareth (Luke 1:26–8). This accomplished, she enquires of the angel: 'How shall be this since a man I know not?' This is a literal rendering of: '*Hos estai touto epei andra ou ginosko?*' which in the Authorized Version appears as 'How shall this be, since I know not a man?' Other translations read: 'How can this be? said Mary; I am still a virgin' (New English Bible, 1970), the 1961 New Testament version of which has '... when I have no husband?'; 'But how can this come about, since I am still a virgin?' (Jerusalem Bible, 1974). These efforts are no improvement on what appears in the Tyndale Bible (1535), Geneva Bible (1562), Rheims Bible (1582), Revised Version (1901), all of which accord with the Authorized (King James) Version. However, the angel's answer: 'The Holy Spirit shall come upon you, and the power of the Most High will overshadow you...' is not mangled in any of these.

Clearly, the rendering 'when I have no husband' in the 1961 New Testament is close, but not close enough, whereas 'I am still a virgin' of the 1970 New English Bible is blatant eisegesis. The Jerusalem Bible's 'How can this come about, since I am a virgin?' is suspiciously similar. This is not what is in the text, and is a good example of rationalization and unnecessary as well as biased paraphrasing. The verb 'to know' has connotations of 'having sexual commerce with', or 'to have carnal knowledge of', albeit in a somewhat archaic sense, but there seems to be scant reason for the translators to take liberties by underlining the general idea that Mary was a virgin; so there must have been a good reason for Luke to write precisely what he did.

From the biblical Scriptures, which themselves harbour much in the way of Mystery knowledge and wisdom, we find this verb actually employed to indicate sexual intercourse. It is noteworthy that 'Adam *knew* Eve his wife, and she conceived and bare Cain, and said, I have gotten a man from the Lord' (Genesis 4:1, cf. 4:25). Accordingly, we find echoes of this event in the New Testament, when, on the occasion of the annunciation, Mary responded to the angel Gabriel's proclamation by asking: 'How can this be, since I *know* not a man?' This phrase is unwittingly apt, and interesting light is thrown on the whole matter by Rudolf Steiner in the booklet *Memory and Habit*: 'In Atlantean times all sexuality was an unconscious process, and various myths and legends of ancient times point to this phenomenon. Only in the course of time was it raised to the realm of consciousness.' The tradition of 'passionless coupling' whereby there was no lust involved nicely echoes this notion.

In the apocryphal Gospel According to the Egyptians, Salome (presumably she who is mentioned in Matthew 15:40 and 16:1, and was evidently a close associate and follower of Christ) was reported by Clement of Alexandria to have asked the Messiah, 'Until when shall men continue to die?' (Strom. III, 9:64) to which he replied: 'So long as women bear children.' When Salome went on to ask when the things concerning which she asked should be known, the Lord said: 'When ye have trampled on the garment of shame, and when the two become one and the male with the female is neither male nor female' (III, 13:92). The so-called Second Epistle of Clement reports something similar, in this case the answer being: 'When the two shall become one, and the outside (that which is without) as the inside (that which is within), and the male with the female neither male nor female' (XII, 2).

This is an obvious reference to the Fall, an outcome of which was that human beings, having been expelled from the Garden as a consequence of eating the fruit of the Tree of the Knowledge of Good and Evil, were now to be subject to birth and death. Heretofore, they had been cherished in the heavenly worlds but at the cost of lacking in self-determination and free will. The Lord God himself made 'coats of skin(s)' for Adam and Eve (Genesis 3:21). Prior to this (Zohar II,

229b) they had 'garments of light'. In the circumstances, therefore, the division into the sexes was inevitable, for how else would earthly bodies be provided for the erstwhile dwellers in the Garden, those spiritual entities which now were obliged to inhabit the earthly world? Henceforward they would be obliged to work for their sustenance, and be subject to decay and death, after which they would abide in the heavenly worlds until the time came for re-embodiment— another birth, and another death, and so on repeatedly, inexorably and indefinitely.

So it was with the first Adam. Salvation could come only by way of the second Adam, whose sacrificial death would atone for all the sins of the first Adam and his earthbound progeny; and this second Adam was to be none other than the Christ. Only with the coming of his kingdom would it be possible once again for the descendants of Adam and Eve to find their way back to a purely spiritual existence, and in doing so lose the necessity for providing earthly bodies. Hence, they would be able to return to their asexual state, which prevailed before the Fall.

Only thus would the inner become the outer in terms of the organs of procreation, and the outer become the inner, the two becoming one. The 'garment of shame' which their pro-genitors had acquired upon the realization that they were naked would then have been well and truly trampled on. The self-consciousness that had been bestowed on them at that time, and had been passed on down through the generations, would be capable of forming the basis for empathic con-sciousness with their fellows. To the *freedom* which they had acquired by reason of their wilfulness would then be added *love*—the selfless, non-possessive *agape* or pure Christian love of self-sacrifice. For this to be achieved, not only was it necessary for the two Jesus boys to become one, but for Jesus of Nazareth and the Christ also to become one. All this finds echoes in Rudolf Steiner's reasons for referring to mankind as the 'Hierarchy of Love and Freedom'.

7
IS A CHILD A 'THING'?

It seems significantly deliberate that Luke, when describing the annunciation scene, worded the angel's answer to Mary's question 'How can this be, since I know not a man?' as: 'The Holy Ghost shall come upon thee, and the power of the Highest shall overshadow thee; therefore also that holy thing (*hagion*) which shall be born of thee shall be called the Son of God' (Luke 1:35). For the most part, this verse has been taken simplistically, and because of its inbuilt implications it seems to propose that it is the Holy Ghost that somehow 'fathers' the 'holy thing' that Mary is carrying. Various published translations come up with the same theme (a child) with slight variations, as in the New English Bible: '... and for that reason the holy child will be called "Son of God" ' (a footnote runs 'Or, the child to be born will be called holy "Son of God" '). The Jerusalem Bible has: 'And the child will be holy and will be called Son of God.' Most Bibles contemporaneous with the Authorized Version also rendered *hagion* as 'thing', not as the euphemistic 'child'—a typical modern example of exegesis overcome by eisegesis.

Now if these interpretations are really what Luke meant to say, why did not he not employ the appropriate word? The Greek word *hagion* is of neuter gender and means some*thing* set apart or separated by or for God, sacred or holy in the very highest degree as well as bearing connotations of utter purity in both spiritual and ceremonial senses. That a pre-pubertal child to be referred to as 'it' is reasonable enough, and indeed common practice, but we soon find out that the gender of this 'child' is 'male'. Things are not as simple as they seem, however. The boy Jesus did not, presumably, grow up to be anything but a man, as Jesus of Nazareth. That is the 'child' matter settled. But where do we find ourselves with respect to the 'Son of God'? Such an exalted being, being necessarily spiritual in character, cannot be assigned to any gender; it is, of course, neuter, thereby qualifying for the use of the word 'thing'.

In the same verse (Luke 1:35) it is mentioned that the 'holy thing' referred to '*shall be* called the Son of God'—not, be it noted, '*is* the Son of God' *already*. That this eventually comes about is made clear in Luke's genealogical table (3:38), so these facts would seem to suggest that the 'holy thing' is undeniably 'of God'. It is probable that Luke made use of this designation simply because of the difficulties involved in identifying this particular entity. Rudolf Steiner, in his lecture course *The Gospel of St Luke* in Bascl, Switzerland, in 1909, made clear what this 'holy thing' was. To the unprepared reader (his hearers would have had little difficulty in understanding it) such a statement sounds outlandish, or even absurd. In his fourth lecture he said: 'Into the child born of the parents called Joseph and Mary in the Gospel of St Luke, there was merged a great individual power which had been carefully preserved and guarded in the great Mother-lodge and Sun-oracle.' Now it was mentioned in the previous paragraph that *hagion* means *something set apart*, and this is precisely what Steiner said concerning it.

As might be expected, from birth this (Luke) Jesus was nurtured in body and soul by his loving and pious mother. At Luke 2:40 we read: 'And the little child grew, and became strong in spirit, being filled with wisdom, and the grace of God was upon him.' At Luke 2:52 we read: 'And Jesus increased in wisdom and stature, and in favour with God and man.' Of this quoted passage Steiner said: 'In truth, this passage stands as follows when we restore the text of the Gospels from the Akashic Records: "The twelve-year-old child increased in all in which an etheric body can increase, namely, all the qualities of kindliness and goodness, and he increased in all in which a physical body can increase, that is to say, in all that pours itself into external beauty of form." '

This statement implies that he was already well advanced, and possessed the potential for what was to follow. After the temple event in his twelfth year he 'increased in wisdom and stature, and in favour (*chariti* = agreeableness, charm) with God and man' (Luke 2:52). These attributes were enhanced after the incident in the temple when he was twelve years old. Rudolf Steiner asserted that this should be understood with reference to the threefold nature of all human beings. The development of the *astral* body, our cognitive principle, alludes to his increase in wisdom. The advancement in stature and in favour with God and with people is clearly to be associated with his *physical* body and the *etheric* or life-body which sustains it. Moreover, it implies the development simultaneously of his pleasing character, built up by the growth in goodness and virtue by dint of his wholesome upbringing by a faithful and devoted mother.

Connections with Zarathustra and the Buddha

It is customary for people to prefer simplicity to complexity, probably because it means an easier life—a state most people aspire to. All too often, however, difficulties arise that cannot be ignored or bypassed merely because they appear to be insoluble. *Credo quia absurdum* (I believe because it is absurd) attributed to Tertullian springs to mind, but Hamlet's rebuttal 'There are more things in heaven and earth, Horatio, than are dreamt of in your philosophy' is equally applicable. What follows promises a testing time.

One might almost believe that there was some kind of connivance between Matthew and Luke in their approach to their Gospels, so beautifully do they complement each other's efforts. Not surprisingly, there is no mention of Zarathustra in Matthew's Gospel and no reference to Gautama Buddha in Luke's, but Steiner, from his researches, fills in the gaps. Just as he contended that the corporeal nature of the Matthew Jesus derived from Zarathustra, known also as Zoroaster, he asserted that the soul-spiritual nature of the Luke Jesus was likewise associated with the Buddha.

Human beings function as a united entity, but they may also be regarded as twofold, threefold, fourfold—even sevenfold and ninefold. However, we are commonly thought of as comprising body and soul, which may be further subdivided respectively into physical and etheric principles as (a) our corporeal nature, and (b) into astral body and ego with regard to our soul-spiritual nature. In terms of evolution, this marked roughly the time of transition from the Middle Stone Age to the New Stone Age, that is to say, between the seventh Atlantean epoch (Indian) and the first post-Atlantean (Persian) epoch (approximately 7000 BC to 5000 BC), when human beings gradually prepared for advancement at a more rapid rate. Previously, our ancestors felt much more integrated into, even in unity with, the outer world than we do now, and the differentiation process was expressed in a greater awareness of both time and space. Their appreciation of time was expressed in the realization of the number seven as being meaningful, gained mainly from their enhanced perception of the starry worlds. It is no coincidence that the year was divided into twelve months, roughly mirroring the zodiac, and the planetary stars the seven (12 × 2-hour) days of the week.

The star mentioned in Matthew's Gospel (2:2–9) was seen 'in the east', which suggests that, seen from the Middle East, it was in the direction of lands further east—Persia, perhaps. Moreover, the name Zoroaster means 'Golden Star', and this is no coincidence. According to Steiner, the original Zarathustra was succeeded over the centuries by other leaders in the name of Zarathustrianism from early post-Atlantean times. It was then that the archetypal formula of dualism became acknowledged, and for the necessity of allowing the new to arise and the old to remain behind. Zarathustra taught that from Time proceeded Ormuzd or Ahura Mazda, the principle of light, to whom was opposed Ahriman or Angra Mainyu, the Lords respectively of Light and Truth, Darkness and Lies. It is significant in archetypal terms that the sun, in its retrogressive path around the earth, was at about that time—approximately 5000 BC to 3000 BC—transiting the zodiacal sign of Gemini, the Twins, the cypher for which is opposing hemispheres representing heaven and earth, separated (or joined) by two pillars, thus ♊. Moreover, it was during this period that the human astral (starry) body was being developed, with its constant oscillation between sympathy and antipathy so characteristic of our (dualistic) soul-life.

As mentioned earlier, it was the individuality of Zarathustra which was incarnated in the body of the Matthew Jesus after 42 generations—from Abraham to Jesus. Matthew was careful to point out (1:17) for the benefit of those who are able to read between the lines, that the list of names is ordered in three blocks of 14. This is no arbitrary arrangement, for it runs parallel to another grouping of 14 × 3, or 7 × 2 × 3, for it has to do with the natural stages of development of (1) the human physical body; (2) the etheric body, and (3) the astral body, as described in Chapter 2. Rudolf Steiner contended that in terms of human descendants, characteristics are not transmitted from one generation to the next, from parents to child, but from grandparents to child, thus as it were leaping those of the immediate predecessor. Moreover, just as the individual undergoes a stage of evolution every seven years, so the whole structure of the physical body improves throughout the generations until the seventh generation, when a certain state of perfection is attained. Thus, it requires 14 generations in all, as every other generation is missed— hence the 7 × 2 = 14 and 14 × 3 = 42 arrangement. In other words, just as the physical attributes need 14 generations to reach a certain evolutionary stage, so normally do the human etheric and astral components.

Matthew brings this fact to notice in order to confirm that only such a body which had undergone 42 stages of development was fit and worthy enough to be capable of sustaining such an advanced personality as Zarathustra. This is the individuality who incarnated in the Matthew Jesus, and later, in his twelfth year, on the occasion of the temple incident, transferred—significantly, after three days—to the Luke Jesus boy. Such transferences are, averred Steiner, far more numerous than generally acknowledged. Such a 'ladder of ascent' of 42 stages to perfection was known and practised by the Essenes, and this led to perfection of the human physical and etheric principles, and these are reflected in the 42 ancestors listed by Matthew.

Complete in itself as this may seem, such an

accomplishment marks the time when all inherited characteristics obtaining at the first stage of the 42 have so to speak worked themselves out, and the series is completed—the stage at which deification could be claimed. The purely human state had, as it were, reached beyond the human into that of superhuman. Earthly concerns are connected with the number seven and its multiples, and 42 + 7 is 49, the number of years acknowledged by the ancient Hebrews as a jubilee year, which bears connotations of completion of the 'old' era and the beginning of a new one. This circumstance is marked, not surprisingly, by Luke at 4:18, making a direct connection with Isaiah 61:1, with Christ Jesus proclaiming that 'this scripture is fulfilled in your ears' (4:21). This statement, astounding as it was, was not fully appreciated at the time, and neither is it now, except by those who energetically work towards such appreciation by earnestly applying themselves to spiritual advancement. John, by stating that 'He came unto his own, and his own received him not' (1:11), shows that he was well aware of the situation, and furthermore also that the 'power to be sons of God' was available to those who take the necessary steps to attain to the stage of becoming 'once-born' referred to in John's Gospel (1:13).

Thus it comes about that the 'lower' corporeal principles of physical and etheric natures reach the peak of perfection, which culminate at the birth of the Matthew Jesus. It is to be expected that he be born into circumstances which befitted his royal heritage, traceable back to such a great and wise king as Solomon. This suggests a rich cultural background appropriate to his mission, and this finds fulfilment in that eventually he, in his future as Jesus of Nazareth, was capable of becoming a learned rabbi who was smart enough to outwit the doctors of the law in the shape of Pharisees, Sadducees and scribes and scholars generally (Matthew 16:1–12; 12:1–9). He was certainly cast in the mould of a wise and influential Zarathustra, with whose individuality he was born. We do not hear nearly so much of Jesus simply as a 'carpenter' as described on church noticeboards. He is referred to as such at Mark 6:3 and Matthew 13:55. Luke seems to have preferred silence regarding the matter, presumably because he knew what was really the case, that is, he was brought up as both rabbi and carpenter. This accords with the usual practice of the time for ministers of religion and other cultured individuals to learn a trade; for example, Paul was a tentmaker (Acts 18:3).

It was inevitable that Luke should complete the picture by referring to the 'higher' soul-spiritual members of Jesus, namely, the astral body and ego, by building on Matthew's substructure of the human 'lower' physical-etheric nature. The scheme of 42 stages (14×3 or 6×7) was from Abraham to David, from David to Jeconiah, and from him to Jesus and Christ. By the same token, but in reverse order, this pattern applies to the human corporeal members (physical and etheric bodies) as a kind of microcosm. For a human being to achieve access to the Mysteries of the starry, cosmic or universal space as macrocosm demands 7×12 stages of 'ascent' as per the Luke account, or rather $11 \times 7 + 1$ stages to achieve total access to its Mysteries. In the words of Rudolf Steiner:

They who are in quest must guide their astral body and ego in this way through eleven times seven stages, and at the twelfth they are in the spiritual world. If Divinity wished to descend and assume a human ego, it would likewise have to pass down through eleven times seven stages. [...] The

Gospels of Luke and Matthew reveal the secrets of initiation, the descent by certain stages of the Divine Spirit into a human individuality, and correspondingly the successive stages by which an individual can reach forth into the cosmos. (*The Gospel of St Matthew*, Lecture 5)

At this juncture a few words with regard to the Buddha are fitting. Born at Kapilavatthu on the Nepal borders in 623 BC and living for 80 years, Siddhartha Gautama was destined to become a world teacher whose message was primarily that of *metta* or loving kindness to all living beings. He was known as being All-Compassionate as well as All-Enlightened, teaching universal brotherhood and peace, and the breaking down of separatism in all its forms. Rudolf Steiner pointed out that the Buddha's ideology of compassion and love arose for the first time in the history of humanity as a human quality. His great contribution to humanity was his *teaching* of a definite philosophy of life and an extended code of ethical behaviour. Buddhism is not a religion, but his Four Noble Truths, Eightfold Path, Ten Commandments, Ten Perfections and numerous other codes of behaviour and discourses in the interests of the furtherance of social harmony are widely regarded as religious tenets to be lived by. On the other hand, what Christ brought is primarily a living *force* or power, not a 'teaching'. The Sermon on the Mount, numerous parables and advice on how to pray can hardly be regarded as such. His only commandment (John 15:12) was 'that ye love one another, as I have loved you', a love that led to his *deed* of self-sacrifice.

By dint of Siddhartha Gautama's elevation from Bodhisattva to Buddha it was no longer necessary for him to undergo another rebirth on earth; instead, he was now free to participate in earthly affairs from the spiritual realms. Steiner confirmed with reference to the Akashic Records that the Buddha appeared to the shepherds in astral form together with the angel of the Annunciation as a 'multitude of (the) heavenly host praising God and saying, Glory to God in the highest, and on earth peace, in people of good will' (Luke 2:13–14).

Normally, after death a person's astral body dissolves into the common cosmic astrality, but in the case of advanced 'perfect' individuals such as the Buddha it remains intact and is called a *Nirmanakaya*. Now we have established that the Jesus born to the Luke parents was the unsullied, 'perfect' being, the *hagion* or 'holy thing' discussed earlier, the first Adam who had not been subject to the Fall. This guarantees the authenticity of the whole matter, as the angel said to Mary, 'this holy thing which shall be born of thee shall be called the Son of God'. This proclamation was confirmed at Luke 3:38: '. . . which was the son of Adam, which was the son of God.' The 'Adam-entity' that remained 'perfect' was born to parents whose pedigree was traceable to God and was therefore fitting for the tasks ahead. By the same token, the perfect astral body in the form of the Nirmanakaya of the Buddha, which appeared with the angel of the annunciation as the 'heavenly host', was perfectly suitable to function as the astral body of the Luke Jesus, and this became the actuality.

Such was the effect of the Luke Jesus taking on the Zarathustra individuality from the Matthew Jesus that the latter died soon after, as did his mother. The Luke Jesus retained his pristine nature which characterized the first Adam before the Fall. He remained untainted by earthly experiences. Needless to say, perhaps, the boy's physical, etheric and astral members remained. Into this ideal human being entered, during his twelfth year, the noble and lofty individuality of Zarathustra or Zoroaster, and this to a degree which was acceptable for Jesus of Nazareth, on the occasion of his baptism by John in the River Jordan, to receive into his three highly developed members the exalted spiritual Being known as the Christ, and his status as Son of God was confirmed.

By making the statements he did, Luke, ever the hint-dropper, does not fail his readers. At 2:40 he has Jesus as a *paidion* (small child) 'strong in spirit', thus giving forceful indication of the latent spirituality that marks the first Adam, pure, innocent and unsullied. This immaculate being was, by God's grace, imbued with universal wisdom and powers of love, evocative of the Buddha's teaching of loving kindness and ethical standards to all people. At 2:52 Luke describes the twelve-year-old Jesus, already 'filled with wisdom', as now 'advancing'—and this by virtue of the worldly-wisdom of Zarathustra, which was the harvest of many incarnations. Such a state of affairs may at first sight seem strange to the point of being bizarre to many people. Suspension of unbelief may well be called for at this point, but Rudolf Steiner took his many responsibilities seriously, and was very careful as to what he said.

8
THE VIRGINAL CONCEPTIONS AS SPIRITUAL EVENTS

John bore witness concerning him, and cried, saying, This was he of whom I spoke: though coming later in time than I, he was in existence before me; he was first and takes precedence over me.

John 1:15

It requires scant consideration to conclude that the Luke Mary was so spiritually advanced that she, during the visitation of the angel at the annunciation, attained a state of illumination at the 'coming upon' by the Holy Spirit (Luke 1:35). After a little more cogitation it becomes reasonable to contend that the controversies regarding 'virgin birth', 'virginal conception' and similar notions were reified, as it were 'materialized' by those who saw fit to externalize the whole event. This is understandable, for the task of making such esoteric or 'hidden' truths clear to the unprepared masses in simple terms would be neither feasible nor desirable. Clues of these deeper meanings and implications seem to have been deliberately sprinkled by the synoptic evangelists, particularly Luke. Written for a more sophisticated readership, John's gospel is richly laced with esoteric truths, and his Book of Revelation even more so.

At Luke 1:31 we read: 'And behold, thou shalt conceive in thy womb, and bring forth a son, and shalt call his name Jesus.' There is no implication here that any conception would be 'of the Holy Spirit', and this is echoed by Matthew at 1:18. There is nothing definite here that infers that her conception was achieved by any other means than normal biological procedures. Indeed, the very mention of 'the Holy Spirit' should alert readers to the understanding that the whole event was of a *spiritual* nature as well as a physical one. This is implicated by Matthew at 1:16, for the birth of his Jesus was listed together with, and by similar procedures, the rest of his ancestors. This simple, straightforward statement is in contradiction with the account of his birth at 1:18–21. However, this is strangely in disparity with the birth of his Jesus as listed with the rest of his ancestors at 1:16. At verse 20 the Greek term *gennethen* is commonly translated as 'conceived' or 'is begotten', but it can also be construed in terms of *spiritual renewal*, with its connotations of rebirth, and some lexicons apply this interpretation to Matthew 1:20 (born of God) as well as to John 1:13 and 1 John 5:1a: '. . . whosoever believeth that Jesus is the Christ is born of God'. The implications with regard to the Holy Spirit are more than hinted at here. It might justifiably be contended that the Matthew Mary was spontaneously 'illuminated' at around this time, as was her namesake in the Luke nativity story with regard to her annunciation event.

Another key word, *apiskiadzo*, is properly rendered as 'overshadow', yet can be regarded also as signifying the presence of a superior factor of some kind, this being the only hint of its active presence. The real meaning of such words with respect to the term 'holy thing' is also baffling—so much so that translators felt obliged to rationalize matters by drawing the 'obvious' conclusion that the holy thing (*hagion*) could not possibly refer to any other 'thing' than a male child in process of being gestated. That the whole matter is unquestionably to do with a 'thing' also seems extraordinary, so that suspicions must arise that Luke is writing for those capable of reading between the lines, as hinted elsewhere. He was enthusiastic about the Holy Spirit, as was his friend and collaborator Paul, and this is worth bearing in mind.

It may well be contended that the Matthew Mary was spontaneously 'illuminated' at around this time (Matthew 1:18, 20), much as her namesake in the Luke nativity story (1:35). It is notable that the term 'over-shadowed' by a cloud is reported on the occasion of the Transfiguration (Matthew 17:5, Mark 9:7, Luke 9:34), Matthew adding that the cloud was 'bright'. That Jesus himself 'charged them (his disciples), saying, Tell the *vision* to no man, until the Son of man be risen again from the dead' attests that the whole event was a clairvoyant experience shared by them all. Moreover, it qualifies for the term 'spiritual renewal' of the previous paragraph, which also denoted significant events.

Nowadays, the prevailing notion, absurd as it is, is that the 'virginal conception' of the Luke Jesus involved physical-material impregnation of Mary by a purely immaterial entity in the form of 'the Holy Spirit'; but the presence of the name Joseph in the genealogical table would affirm that the fathering procedure involved him too. Common sense, as well as common science, maintains that matter can only procreate matter, as likewise spirit can only beget spirit. Luke 1:35 does not make it clear, in the absence of the definite article, but (The or A or neither) 'Spirit holy shall come upon thee...' must stand as is. However, '*the* holy thing shall be called Son of God' nevertheless—but what is this 'holy thing'? (See Chapter 7.) The wording '*the*' seems already to anticipate the Trinity, which has its roots in the event of the baptism of Jesus of Nazareth in the River Jordan when 'he saw the spirit of God descending as a dove, and coming upon him, and lo, a

voice out of the heavens, saying "This is my Son..."'
(Matthew 3:16, Mark 1:10, 11), Luke 3:22, John 1:32–34).
Matthew employs *ginomai*, which has overtones of 'become,
pass from one state to another, be born'. Mark chose
erxomenon—the 'coming one', i.e. the Messiah; John has
emeinen—abode (on). These slight differences are interesting,
and support the notion that the four evangelists 'saw' the
Baptismal event clairvoyantly, for it is certain that none of
them was actually present at the time.

This kind of language, strange as it may seem in our
modern intellectual age, is in fact quite articulate. There can,
of course, be no question of conception in any other mode but
the purely natural one, but the symbolism is nonetheless
discernible. The whole affair was externalized or reified for
apprehension by *hoi polloi*, ordinary people to whom the
Mysteries were closed, but effectively presenting to them what
was really a spiritual event into the more familiar and
ordinary physical one. That the events concerning both
Marys became materialized and consequently rigidified into
dogma is not surprising: the seeds of the (Luke) 'Mary cult'
which was to follow had been sown.

John, at 3:6, has Christ Jesus himself saying, 'That which
has been born of the flesh, flesh is; and that which has been
born of the spirit, spirit is', a statement which should give
serious thought to the 'virginal conceptionists'. But all this
is not only merely a matter of semantics, but also of the
manner in which ancient writers often expressed concepts in
figurative or metaphorical terms. Who would categorically
declare that the 'Lamb of God' was a divine juvenile sheep,
or that 'the valley of the shadow of death' could be found
on the map?

In this respect it is worth noting that such illumination or revelation was experienced by numerous New Testament characters. Such references indicate the manifestation of either spontaneous or acquired supersensible perception or—to use a much misapplied term—clairvoyance, in such diverse individuals as Elizabeth, Simeon, Zacharias, Stephen, Peter, Barnabas and Paul. Some were true 'initiates' with reliable and consistent powers of spiritual perception, while for others their experiences were more likely to be involuntary revelation. The very word *initiate* is abhorrent to those who confine themselves to belief only, which may or may not accord with reality. It smacks too much of the ancient 'pagan' Mysteries; but some of these were Christian through and through. Closely related to these matters is that of individuals being born again, born of God, born of the spirit, 'twice-born' and suchlike. A good example of this kind of thing is the story at John 3:1, 13 involving the visit by Nicodemus to Jesus 'by night'—a revelatory experience indeed—a conversation well worth overhearing.

Developing our latent powers

It must never be forgotten that 'God is a spirit, and they who worship Him must worship Him in Spirit and in truth' (John 4:24). As has been vouchsafed all along, we humans are primarily spiritual beings, and only secondarily are we beings of flesh and blood. It is therefore perfectly right and proper that we seek whatever is of the spirit, and 'work out our own salvation with fear and trembling' (Philippians 2:12). Those who are 'drawn', in the sense of John 6:44, with all the earnestness and zeal of the Medieval mystics, seek to return to their very source in the Godhead. However, as we know, the route to this source is to be reached only by way of the Son,

Christ Jesus himself, the purveyor of grace and truth (John 1:14).

It is reasonable to postulate that this is the second step, the first being via the Holy Spirit: 'He (the Son) shall baptize you with the Holy Ghost, and with fire' (Matt 3:11; Mark 1:8; Luke 3:16; John 1:33). Thus we have all four evangelists declaring that those who aspire to spiritual heights shall first be baptized by none other than the Holy Spirit. We read that 'baptism with the Holy Spirit' is promised to the apostles (Acts 1:5), and at 1:8 that they 'shall receive power, after that the Holy Spirit is come upon (them)...' which they did at the time of Pentecost (Acts 2:1–4). Ideally, it is only after such a 'baptism of fire' by the agency of the Holy Spirit that the first step is to be taken.

Needless to say, the 'Sonship' of Christ Jesus was authenticated by the event of his baptism in the River Jordan by John at 1:32–34: 'I have beheld the Spirit descending as (or like as) a dove out of heaven, and it abode upon him. And I knew not him; but he who sent me to baptize with water, he to me said, Upon whom thou shalt see the Spirit descending and abiding on him, he it is who baptizes with the Holy Spirit. And I have seen, and have borne witness that this is the Son of God.' This episode appears in somewhat different terms in Matthew (3:16, 17), Mark (1:8–11) and Luke (3:22), although Luke is the only evangelist who states what may already be understood, namely that the man who was baptized was 'the Son of God' who was begotten on that day. The New English Bible reports, much to the satisfaction of all Adoptionists: 'Some witnesses read, My Son art thou; this day have I begotten thee'.

All this means that at the baptism two significant occurrences were made manifest: firstly, Jesus of Nazareth was authoritatively 'adopted' by God (the Father) at that particular time, and secondly that the occasion was marked by the 'sending' of the Holy Spirit to his Son. Thus the Son, being now indwelt by the Holy Spirit, is empowered or commissioned to bestow the same tribute on his disciples, who at the event of Pentecost were authorized by God to 'pour out' his Spirit 'upon all flesh'.

The event of Pentecost was preceded by 'a sound from heaven as of a rushing mighty wind (*pnoes biaias*—literally 'violent breath'), and this is somewhat reminiscent of *pneuma* (air in motion, wind, vital spirit), as in *pneuma hagion* (spirit holy) of the annunciation event at Luke 1:35. It almost seems that Luke is trying to associate these two events, applying the highly symbolic language also employed by all other New Testament contributors. The (or A) Holy Spirit is as it were present at the 'heralding' of the Matthew Jesus and also of his ascension—entry into the world and departure from it. The whole situation was succinctly put by Rudolf Steiner in these words:

At the dawn of Christianity the communication of the Holy Spirit and the manifestation of the Holy Spirit at the Baptism—this was the deed of the Father. The sending of the Holy Spirit to His disciples—this was the deed of Christ, of the Son. Therefore, it was ancient dogma that the Father is the Uncreated Creator, the Son is created by the Father; the Holy Spirit is the principle communicated to mankind by the Father and the Son. This is not dogma arbitrarily formulated: it is Initiation-Wisdom of the earliest Christian centuries, and it was shattered only in later times.

For the first four centuries AD there was wide acceptance that knowledge of the supersensible realms was as valid as that of the material world—if anything more so. One has only to think, compared with modern times, just how extremely limited knowledge of the material world was. Nowadays, the science of natural phenomena and their workings is so vast that it has to be compartmentalized into numerous disciplines, which are further split into specialisms. Moreover, positivism—belief that sense-perceptions are the only admissible basis for human knowledge and precise thought, and as such is entirely materialistic—is a widespread dogma. Such a tenet obviously utterly denies any validity for religious beliefs: the concept of 'spirit' is therefore meaningless to materialist scientists. Needless to say, the weakness of religious beliefs is that they rely for the most part on faith alone, and this establishes their inadequacy. However, the work of spiritual investigators such as Rudolf Steiner have succeeded in establishing a whole well-structured, reliable and valid *science of the spirit*, every bit as authentic as modern natural science. Moreover, Steiner has demonstrated that it is possible to transmute modern intellectual knowledge into spiritual knowledge.

CONCLUSION

Rudolf Steiner, in the first lecture of his course *The Gospel of St John* held at Kassel (24 June–7 July 1909), made it clear that 'whatever is real and true must ever and again be proclaimed in new forms and in new ways, for the requirements of humanity alter from epoch to epoch. Our time needs a new annunciation of this greatest of events in the history of mankind'. He went on to declare that the deliberate making public of anthroposophical spiritual science is new only in respect of its form. He contended that spiritual investigators throughout the ages have confirmed from their own experience *for the benefit of mankind* that our highest spiritual principle whilst on the earthly plane, namely, our higher ego—which never leaves the spiritual world—is capable of being as it were born, as a child is born of a mother. Such an event, which in effect allows of access to the spiritual realms, is the result of what is commonly referred to as awakening, enlightenment, rebirth, initiation, 'Damascus experience'.

It bears repetition that the originator of Christianity, the Christ Being, was 'born' in Jesus of Nazareth on the occasion of his baptism in the River Jordan: 'Thou art my Son, my Beloved; this day I have begotten thee.' This spiritual event was enacted for the benefit of the whole of mankind *as historical fact*, and therefore one of cosmic and earthly significance alike, particularly with regard to the Fall and the possibility of redemption. There is more than a hint of parallelism here. Simply put, in terminology that is unquestionably metaphorical, God 'sent' his 'only-begotten Son' (John 1:18), thus employing images of 'birth' and parenthood—

particularly motherhood. In consequence we have icons of mother and child. Long before the advent of the Christ on earth, figures representative of mother and child were common 'visual aids' for the neophytes in the Mystery Centres of the Near and Middle East. Thus did the concept of a real live mother and child arise as material icons for the masses, all in the best of faith and earnest good will, to apprehend what was a spiritual reality.

The Christ was 'born' of God, and through his crucifixion and resurrection he became the Redeemer of 'the fallen'. 'But as many as received him, gave he power to become the sons of God, even to them that believe on his name: Which were born, not of blood, nor of the will of the flesh, nor of the will of man, but of God' (John 1:12–13). This makes matters clear, inasmuch as those who 'receive' him into themselves qualify to be reckoned as 'sons (children) of God'. The prerogative thus to receive him rests with each individual. We must as it were give birth to the Christ within ourselves, and this within our highest spiritual member, namely, the ego. Christ Jesus had come to 'take away the sin of the world', declared John (1:29). This sin is that of *human egotism*. Reflection will confirm that, in the last resort, every act of evil, whatever leads to corruption, is traceable to self-indulgence. It is also noteworthy that the last petition in the Lord's Prayer is that we be 'delivered from evil', or more correctly 'that-which-is evil', which is our greatest enemy and manifests as our inclination for egotism. The panacea for this is *love*.

SELECT BIBLIOGRAPHY

Books by Rudolf Steiner (Rudolf Steiner Press, UK, or Steiner Books, USA)

A Road to Self-knowledge
The Fifth Gospel
The Christian Mystery in Relation to the Secret of Pentecost
From Jesus to Christ
Mystery Centres
Verses and Meditations
The Christian Mystery
Christianity as Mystical Fact
Christianity and the Mysteries of Antiquity
The Effects of Esoteric Development
Knowledge of the Higher Worlds
The Way of Self-knowledge
Mystery of the Universe
Memory and Habit
The History of the Earth and the Spiritual Victory over the Sun
The Gospel of St John and its Relation to the Other Gospels
The Gospel of St Luke
The Gospel of St Matthew
Christ and the Human Soul
The Birth of Christ in the Human Soul

Books by other authors

Young, J.,   *Know Your Faith in a Decade of Evangelism*

Reisenman, R.,   *James, the Brother of Jesus*
Josephus, F.   *Antiquities of the Jews*
Reitenstein, R.,   *The Hellenistic Mystery-Religions*
Wand, W.J.C.,   *A History of the Early Church until*
                        AD *500*
Scholem, G.,   *The Messianic Idea in Judaism*
Brown, R.,   *The Birth of the Messiah*
Binz, S.J.,   *The Advent of the Savior*
Krause-Zimmer, H.,   *Die Zwei Jesusknaben in der bildenen*
                        Kunst
Peake's Commentary on the Bible

Apocryphal books:
The Gospel of Thomas
The Gospel of the Hebrews
Wisdom of Solomon
The Book of Enoch
Gospel According to the Egyptians
The Second Epistle of Clement